DEALING WITH CHANGE IN YOUR PERSONAL LIFE

Battle Your Fear of Change and Realize Opportunities for Growth

ALEX HAYDON

© **Copyright 2021 - All rights reserved.**

The content contained within this book may not be reproduced, duplicated or transmitted without direct written permission from the author or the publisher.

Under no circumstances will any blame or legal responsibility be held against the publisher, or author, for any damages, reparation, or monetary loss due to the information contained within this book, either directly or indirectly.

Legal Notice:

This book is copyright protected. It is only for personal use. You cannot amend, distribute, sell, use, quote or paraphrase any part, or the content within this book, without the consent of the author or publisher.

Disclaimer Notice:

Please note the information contained within this document is for educational and entertainment purposes only. All effort has been executed to present accurate, up-to-date, reliable, complete information. No warranties of any kind are declared or implied. Readers acknowledge that the author is not engaged in the rendering of legal, financial, medical or professional advice. The content within this book has been derived from various sources. Please consult a licensed professional before attempting any techniques outlined in this book.

By reading this document, the reader agrees that under no circumstances is the author responsible for any losses, direct or indirect, that are incurred as a result of the use of the information contained within this document, including, but not limited to, errors, omissions, or inaccuracies.

ISBN is: 9781739924812

Contents

Introduction	v
1. WHAT IS CHANGE (AND WHY ARE YOU AFRAID OF IT)?	1
2. A GLOSSARY OF FEARS RELATED TO CHANGE	15
Change	16
Loneliness	17
Failure	19
Rejection	20
Uncertainty	21
Calamity	22
Pain	23
Judgment	25
Inadequacy	26
Freedom	27
Fear Street	28
3. HINDSIGHT 20/20	31
One	32
Two	33
Three	34
Four	35
Five	36
4. MAKE THE CHANGE AGAINST FEAR OF CHANGE	39
Step 1: Courage	39
Step 2: Humility	42
Step 3: Accountability	44
Step 4: Negativity	46
Step 5: Growth	47
Step 6: Ego	49

5. WHEN FACING CHANGE, COURAGE IS YOUR BEST FRIEND	53
The Leader and the Follower	62
It's a Bit Risky, Don't You Think?	63
6. HUMILITY IN YOUR HEART	71
Not a Weakness	74
7. THE RESPONSIBLE WAY – BE ACCOUNTABLE	81
It Starts with You	82
8. NAVIGATING THROUGH NEGATIVITY	91
A Sense of Fatigue and Hopelessness	97
Excess Of Stress	98
Anxiety Variety	101
That's An Imposter	107
9. AS YOU GROW, YOU EXPERIENCE LIFE	115
Change vs. Growth	115
10. DON'T LET YOUR EGO EMPOWER YOU	123
Conclusion	131
References	135

Introduction

Within you lies an ember.

This ember is a representation of your goal. It isn't too hot; perhaps just comfortably warm. After all, it is something that you would like to do, but you don't have a lot of ideas to latch on to. You don't have a plan, nor a strategy to progress. You might not even have the necessary knowledge to support you in making your next moves.

In short, you want to do something, but you have no idea how to do it. Yet it's a goal that you truly desire. Maybe you would like to purchase a new home. Perhaps you wanted a raise in your job or would like to start your own business. It could even be that you would like to graduate from university with distinction, finish a personal project, buy an expensive vehicle. Or you might have one of the thousands of other goals that people all around the world carry with them every day.

But nothing ever happens.

Introduction

You might find yourself becoming listless as you imagine all the wonderful things that could happen to you if you accomplished your goal. It could be fame, money, love, progress, power, peace, or anything else that you seek. However, that's where your goals end – inside your imagination. They never manifest into reality. You might have sometimes caught yourself in a dreary state, fearing what's to come or what might happen if you started pursuing your goal. You find yourself unable to take action, worrying yourself to distraction about what is to come or what may go wrong.

Science, thankfully, has an understanding of this behavior. Remember those New Year's goals that many people plan to achieve? They become excited and eager for January 1 to arrive, knowing that it's the beginning of a new version of them. Yet according to Harvard Business Review, only a measly 19% of people manage to achieve those goals over the span of the next two years of their lives (Yang et al.).

What does that mean? Let me give you an example. Let's say that you had decided to work out a lot more and develop six-pack abs like those Hollywood megastars who seem to have bodies chiseled by the gods themselves. But according to that Harvard Business Review research, you will more than likely change your goal without achieving it within the next two years. In other words, 19% of people will move on from their original goal without achieving it.

It's a tragedy that we are creatures of comfort. Don't just take my word for it. According to researchers from Simon Fraser University, human beings are wired to be lazy (BBC). We are energy savers, not energy spenders. Even when performing a task, we try to find the easiest way to reach a certain result. It's no wonder that we become paralyzed with fear, confusion, apprehension, or even frustration when we set out to follow our goals.

I can relate. I can understand the need (or feeling, however false it might be) to do something right this moment, before the sands of time slip between our fingers. I didn't have any grand epiphanies or revelations; in fact, I spent 10 years in a job that I very badly wanted to quit. That should probably tell you a lot about how unsure I was about actually starting something on my own.

I went through all the excuses that I could possibly give myself to justify my actions. I blamed it on the economy. Other times, it was the fact that the workload had increased (well, this was partially true, but it wasn't enough to distract me entirely) or that I needed to conduct more research before I attempted to do anything else (the research never happened).

You see, I have always been fascinated by the idea of starting my own motivational program. I knew I had the skills and experiences to connect with a lot of people. However, rather than use the opportunity to explore ideas and trends and conduct a deep study of the market or how to actually go about establishing my name, I just kept pondering about the "what if" situations.

I'm sure you might have had moments like this where you pondered one or several "what if" questions when it came to thinking about your goals or aspirations.

What if things don't go your way? What if you fail? What if your plan is worthless?

In my case, there were plenty of those questions, but the most pressing was:

Introduction

What if I go broke?

From that point onwards I started to become quite miserable. There I was, having tunnel vision that focused on the problems, but that failed to consider or support my skills and my passion. It's like getting yourself an expensive vehicle but rather than driving it, you only think about car accidents, and so you end up not making use of it or taking advantage of it at all. My vehicle was my goal, but I had barely even gotten into the driver's seat.

Then came the depression. My life had reached stagnation, and the lack of progress made me evaluate myself in a poor light. I felt like a failure. I disliked the idea of waking up in the morning, because that meant I had to go back to a job that didn't offer me any joy. I started performing poorly at work. To combat my lackluster performance, I began working even more. I thought that by adding more hours, I would compensate for the mistakes I had made. Little did I know the monster I was creating in my life.

The long hours would further affect my mental health, pushing me deeper into melancholy. That would, in turn, force me to ignore my private life and jump into work as though it was a lifeline I was holding on to. My relationship began to feel the pressure of my decisions. I would avoid chores, shun responsibilities, and just felt lethargic most of the time.

Thankfully, I had people to wake me up to reality. With the support of my friends and family over the course of nearly seven months, I realized that in order to change anything, I needed to let go of my long-held beliefs, habits, and other unhelpful ideas that were holding me down. I needed to change. I couldn't complain about the path ahead if I hadn't even taken a step forward.

Introduction

I finally mustered up the courage to chase my goals with passion and intentional diligence. I couldn't have done it alone, though, but I was lucky to have the right kind of people around me.

I want to be that person for you – that friend who is going to tell you to wake up because you are not done yet. Your goal awaits; all you have to do is make the right decisions. I know you may not be feeling the spark of motivation within you, but you will discover it soon. I will do my best to guide you towards the things that you want and attempt to get you out of your shell with a sense of vigor. I would like to show you how to face your fears and overcome your mental blocks.

The road ahead is going to be tough, but then again, the things we want in life rarely come to us easily. However, with this in mind, it's comforting to know that through your effort and perseverance, you can yield optimal results and turn your life around for the better. This book offers a variety of practical tips and advice to help you do just that.

1

What Is Change (and Why Are You Afraid of It)?

Change is inevitable, everyone knows that.

There's no guarantee that what you are used to right now is going to last for a long time. If you think that you have grown accustomed to or comfortable with something, then you should also know that there are forces out there that can disrupt your life, the kind of forces that are beyond our control. From natural disasters to unexpected personal events, there are threats in our environment that can alter our lives.

A simple example of change is the one that takes place in your body – it grows old, and there is no stopping it. You could exercise and eat healthy every day to make yourself look younger, but your biological clock always ticks away. Apart from the obvious physiological changes, your responsibilities also shift tracks. When we were younger, all we had to worry about was homework, what plans we had to make on the weekends with our friends, getting into a little trouble here and there, and making sure we stuffed ourselves with as much junk food as possible. As adults, we are now concerned about bills, job status, life goals, family, health, the economy, the fact that our favorite TV series has been cancelled, and other adult problems. No matter who you are, you will go through this change. Some people choose to avoid it, doing nothing as they simply continue to exist. Others decide that they are going to make something of their lives and grasp the responsibilities that are part and parcel of the opportunities that come their way.

Here is the important part about this whole experience of growing up into responsibilities: it doesn't go away. It's going to happen, but it's entirely up to you whether you would like to embrace it or ignore it. Either way, it's like a sentient being with a mind of its own. No matter how much you would like to, you can't avoid its existence.

So, what exactly is this persistent phenomenon that we call 'change'?

According to The Merriam-Webster Dictionary, change occurs when someone or something undergoes substitution, transition, or transformation (Merriam-Webster). It relates to a difference that mildly or greatly differs from an original state or existence.

You might perhaps have heard of the saying, "The only constant in life is change."

When I was at my lowest point and my friends were trying to get me back on my feet, I remember one of them saying, "This is not going to stay the same. It will pass." I understood the meaning of his words and realized that he was right. Perhaps I was so hung up on my own problems that I was ignoring the opportunities around me. Sure, at that point in my life, it seemed as though my misfortunes would never end and that I

What Is Change (and Why Are You Afraid of It)?

was doomed to continue my life in perpetual misery and tragedy. However, I began to truly listen to my friend's advice. He was right; change *is* the only constant in life.

But what does that phrase really mean?

Well, to answer that, you merely have to look around you. The world continues to develop and transform. Technological changes allow us to enjoy more comforts and conveniences. Political changes either make or break a country's economy. Social changes instill values and norms that guide us in our interactions with others. Yet they are always going through changes. Five years ago, you probably never imagined that things would be the way they are right now. In fact, five years ago, you likely would never have imagined that a group of microorganisms would actually bring the entire world to a slow crawl and that – at least as of this moment in July of 2021 – there are no known vaccines or treatments for its latest strain.

It's quite something, isn't it? You might imagine that these kinds of events only ever happen in movies. But here we are.

This is a form of change as well. As more and more changes happen around you, whether on a macro scale that affects a lot of people or on a micro scale that impacts only you, you will realize something important: because change occurs constantly, change itself becomes a constant.

It's a bit of an oxymoron, but essentially the phrase "change is the only constant in life" means that change itself becomes continuous. Constant. Never ceasing.

In other words, we can't avoid it. Sure, you can try to pretend it isn't there, but it is going to affect you regardless. It's for this reason that we should actually welcome change into our lives.

DEALING WITH CHANGE IN YOUR PERSONAL LIFE

If we are going to deal with it one way or the other, then why try to fight it? However, that is easier said than done, of course.

As human beings, we become attached to routines, objects, people, and even our environment. We find comfort in familiarity, and that allows us to put a lot of our processes onto autopilot. After all, it's one less thing to worry about. We become comfortable with the way things are because we are used to them.

Any disruption of these routines or familiar presences in our lives causes us to leave our comfort zones. We are forced to take action in an unfamiliar situation or location. It could be something small, such as the power going off in your home, causing you to become frustrated at the government, the weather, or the power company. Or it could be a major incident, such as changing locations because of your career.

All of these changes push us away from our comfort zone. When I say comfort zone, I'm not referring to a physical space or location. Far from it. According to Merriam-Webster, a comfort zone refers to a certain level where one can function with familiarity and ease (Merriam-Webster, "Definition of COMFORT ZONE"). It's a state of existence that allows you to experience a certain level of comfort.

Perhaps psychology has a better way of looking at the idea of a comfort zone, referring to it as a psychological state where individuals experience familiar stimuli that cause them to be at ease (Mead). For example, your daily visits to the local coffee shop before you head to work, or the kind of music you play when you are busy doing something. Even the way you tap your feet when your mind wanders, or you become restless is a familiar movement. Your comfort zone is more a mental state of being in which you rely on a consistent string of habits and patterns that soothe and make things easy or pleasurable for you.

But what happens when this familiarity is removed from our lives? What happens when we have to face an entirely alien or novel situation? Or perhaps when we come face-to-face with something that isn't entirely unfamiliar, but isn't part of our comfortable routine?

In such situations when change does eventually occur, we experience chaos. We panic, become frustrated or upset, or sometimes even disappointed. We fear what we do not know, or any bumps in the road that might inconvenience us or force us to do some problem-solving on the spot.

According to Harvard Business Review, people reject change for only a few vital reasons (Kanter 2018). One of them is the degree of uncertainty that they might face in the future. When we go through life, we are often subjected to various challenges. Some of these challenges end up giving us a victory, but most of them serve as failures. Such failures make us wiser and smarter, give us insights into various situations, showing us that not everything is so black-and white, but more complex and nuanced. They show us how to be more compassionate or empathetic, or they teach us what we shouldn't be doing. However, they also have another unpredictable outcome.

They lower our propensity to take risks.

The more we avoid risks in our lives, the more we begin to fear losing control. After all, when we are facing a familiar situation, we are able to exert a certain level of control over the things that we want to do. Getting your food delivered from your favorite restaurant gives you a sense of control over the situation. You feel as though you have made a decision on what you like to eat, and you know what the outcome will be. However, take away that familiar option, and put yourself in a position where you have to order from an unknown restaurant where you don't know if the food is good and whether you will like the way they prepare the dishes. You might then find yourself feeling at a loss of control over your decisions. This also explains another reason why you prefer the familiar over the alien; the fear of the unknown.

The unknown is a strange place to be. It's like walking blindfolded to the edge of a cliff; you are uncertain about when the drop might occur. In a similar way, the unknown presents you with a set of problems, and you are not sure when you might face them or in what form they might occur. You can definitely prepare yourself, but there are many unknown variables to consider. This situation frightens us, and therefore does not encourage us to progress in our lives. Perhaps it's for that reason that we often continue to exist in misery and tragedy rather than actually doing something about it. People continue to labor away in the same job even though they can clearly see the detrimental effect it is having on their health and wellbeing. Of course, I was partly referring to myself with the previous statement. After all, I had spent nearly ten years hoping that things might get better eventually on their own without any effort on my part.

However, life is an ever-evolving entity; it doesn't stick to any rules. It can meander and flow in different directions. Often, it doesn't even give you a warning in advance, it just does what it has to do. Many of life's changes are unpredictable. They are obstacles that, if not dealt with, might just grow in difficulty or intensity.

It is because of this level of unpredictability and uncertainty that we often avoid change like our lives depend on it. In fact, according to psychologists, one of the core reasons why we avoid change is because we cannot predict the outcome (Razzetti 2018).

Moreover, the level of unpredictability means that we could potentially experience more loss than we had anticipated. For that reason, no one likes to suffer any loss at all. Furthermore, they also don't like to lose something that belongs to them. Whatever kind of loss they experience, they would much rather keep it to an absolute minimum, if they cannot avoid it completely. As a result, people resort to living within the comfortable and mundane because it means they are not risking anything.

We also have little control over future events, and this can be quite disconcerting. You don't know whether your actions are going to be beneficial or if they are going to lead you to failure. For example, if you're planning to apply for a new job, then you're not certain whether you will get an interview or if you are going to face rejection. Among other factors, this lack of control over outcomes keeps people from actually welcoming change.

Let's not forget the degree of confusion you might experience when dealing with change. When an economy crashes, for example, it leaves you in a state of confusion. You would never imagine that things would turn out the way they did, and you're left wondering what you can do or what steps you can take next. It's jarring and overwhelming. You feel lost and it also makes you feel less competent than you actually are. You tend to see yourself in an unfavorable light, and that is definitely a demotivating situation to be in. Who likes to think of themselves as incapable?

However, it's interesting to note that we are focusing on change, but not actually focusing on some of the mental processes that lead to an avoidance or ignorance of that change. In order to truly grasp our mental machinations, we need to delve deeper into our minds. More specifically, we need to enter the realm of the subconscious, where more processes take place than we might realize at first.

As human beings, we generally like to feel that we are in power and that we are consciously able to make the decisions that affect us. We believe that we are always aware of our actions and can, at any time, quickly perform a course-correct to change what we are going to do or say or think. However, science has proven otherwise.

In order to fully grasp the true power of the subconscious mind, we need to look at the way we make our purchase decisions. Yes, you read that right; I want to talk about the things that you buy. How do you do it? Take five minutes to truly think about your buying process. Where does it start? What makes you spend your hard-earned money on a particular service or product? Who or what influences your purchase decisions? Most importantly, *are* you consciously making a decision on how you should spend your money?

According to Gerald Zaltman, professor at Harvard Business School, in his book *How Customers Think: Essential Insights into the Mind of the Market* (Zaltman and Harvard Business Press), our subconscious mind makes 95% of our purchase decisions. That's a surprisingly high percentage. If I had told you that your subconscious mind makes 64% of the purchase decisions, you might be surprised, but not very. You might eventually feel as though your conscious mind is at least in control of a large portion of your decisions. But 95%? That's quite something, isn't it!

I would like you to try out an activity right now, as you are reading this book.

I would like you to focus on these words. Truly focus on them. Quite frankly, there isn't anything special about them. You could try and check to see if I am hiding some meaning or code in the arrangement of words you see before you, but I assure you that there is nothing mysterious at play. Now, you might be wondering if this is one elaborate prank to throw you off. It is not. You might now wonder how long I am going to keep this exercise going. That is indeed a good question. The answer is quite simple: I'm going to stop the exercise right about now.

Did you notice something?

If you did, what was it that you noticed?

Let me say this; it isn't necessarily about what you noticed, but about what you didn't.

While you were reading that fairly confusing paragraph earlier, did you notice your rate of breathing? How about your body's posture? What about the room's temperature? How about that important task for tomorrow? Is the lighting in your room perfect? What about the position of your arms and legs?

All of the little sensations that you don't pay attention to are managed by your subconscious. You go through this process every day, when you're driving in the car or walking home from work, when performing a chore or playing a video game.

When you are focused on a task, you put many of your actions into automation. Let's talk about the aforementioned example of driving your car. You could put each and every microdecision into your conscious mind – the turning of the wheel, the movement of your feet as you shift gears, the movement of your eyes as you glance at the mirror, the shift in your body posture as you make yourself comfortable, and the dozens of other decisions that are needed to avoid bumping into another vehicle.

Or you could rely on your subconscious's muscle memory and turn up the radio, tapping your fingers on the wheel to your favorite tune as you focus on your destination.

That's right, muscle memory is in your head and not in your body (Shusterman). It is your subconscious mind telling your body what to do.

So why are we talking about the subconscious mind? It's because of a wonderful psychological phenomenon called priming. According to researchers from the University of Toronto, priming is a phenomenon in which a preexisting stimulus affects emotions, decisions, ideas, or stimuli in the present (Tulving and Schacter 1990). This phenomenon occurs when we are not consciously aware of it. In other words, it's an automatic response.

Think about the first thing that you do when you wake up in the morning. It could be brushing your teeth or a quick warm-up exercise. Maybe you might gulp down a glass of water. No matter what you do, the action is automatic. You didn't consciously initiate the thought that you should go and take care of the first activity. It just popped into your head.

What Is Change (and Why Are You Afraid of It)?

Think about the other cues you receive throughout your day. Before you start work, you grab a cup of coffee. Sure, you might think that you voluntarily decided to get your hot beverage in the morning, but are you truly aware of the inception of the idea?

We could even examine your personal preferences. Why do you like one brand of electronics over another? What if there are better options out there? Why do you like the color red or chocolate flavored ice cream? Your likes and dislikes, and even your preferences, are all emotionally charged. This means that you have an emotional attachment to certain preferences in your life. But if I were to ask you why you prefer that, you might come up with a reason. You might throw in some cool features about your choice. Perhaps you would talk about why many other people also share your preferences. But in the end, it's simply because of your emotional attachment towards that object, idea, or option that you tend to navigate towards it.

This emotional attachment cannot be easily explained. It is present deep within your subconscious. This is what priming is; suggestions that are established deep within the subconscious that become activated when you perform a certain action, experience a certain emotion, or face a situation.

More importantly, your subconscious is emotional. It reacts based on your previous experiences and preexisting ideas. In contrast, the conscious part of your brain is the rational one, able to analyze facts and figures in order to come to a logical conclusion.

But why is it important to understand the subconscious mind and the fact that it is the emotional part of our brain? I'm going to get to that in a moment. Before that, however, I would like to bring up an interesting discovery that was made in the 1980s by neuroscientist Benjamin Libet (Douglas 2010). He asked a subject to twitch his finger and then tried to capture the reaction by analyzing brain activity. What he discovered was quite surprising. Libet noticed a burst of brain activity 300 milliseconds before the subject consciously chose to twitch the finger.

In other words, the subject had subconsciously made the decision before even becoming consciously aware of it.

We, as human beings, like to believe that we are always making decisions consciously. But that's not true. We rely on the subconscious mind more than we realize. The more we rely on our subconscious, the more we use the phenomenon of priming. By taking an additional 15 minutes to wake up in the morning after the alarm has gone off, we are primed to hit the snooze button and head back to bed in the future. Our dietary choices, work ethics, personality quirks, and even our preferences are all created through priming because of our reliance on our subconscious minds.

Do note that the subconscious mind isn't a villain. It's not some kind of boogeyman that you need to be worried about. On the contrary, it is a vital component of the human experience. Think of it this way; when you wake up in the morning, do you really want to spend the next 15 minutes consciously managing each and every decision you make? These decisions include moving your legs, opening the curtains, lifting your arms above your head to stretch, taking deep breaths, adjusting your posture, wiggling your toes, the movement of your feet as you walk, the way you breathe, and other small actions. Or would you rather have all of the small actions put into automation as you ponder your goals, schedules, and other important plans you have made for the day?

The subconscious is an important component of your existence. However, things don't tend to take a turn for the better when you start to rely on it too much. Most of the things you do, experience, and feel are recorded by your subconscious and used to influence you in the future. The reason why you procrastinate a lot? Priming. Why do you get upset over little things when they are not worth losing your temper over? Again, priming. Do you give up easily on your goals when you experience even the smallest of challenges? Oh look, it's your friend priming again.

Over the course of your life, you have subconsciously convinced yourself that you are lazy, a smoker, lacking self-confidence, not capable of greatness, or the countless other negative ideas or beliefs you fill yourself with. In the same way, you have convinced yourself that you are not someone who likes change, that you cannot handle change, that you are afraid of the unknown, that there is no way you can find the courage to face your fears and take on challenges. You have convinced yourself that between being the hero or the villain of the story, you are probably that extra who gets killed off in the first few minutes of the movie; someone inconsequential.

Yet, all of this is in your head. You're not afraid of change; you *think* you are afraid of change. In fact, neuroscience has discovered that one of the ways to treat a range of mental health problems is through the use of cognitive behavioral therapy (Hofmann et al. 2012), which is quite literally a technique used to reprogram your mind. Such techniques are also used to treat fears and other debilitating mental conditions. The reality is that scientists have discovered that all your apprehensions and worries start in your head. The more you exercise them, the more they manifest themselves as behavioral patterns, and the more you accept them as something you *are* rather than something you *do*.

Eventually, those behavioral patterns can be detrimental to your growth, such as that of avoiding change.

Since we are on the subject of fear, let's try exploring that further.

2

A Glossary of Fears Related to Change

Fear. A pesky little thing, isn't it?

From the little things, like worrying about what you might face in the dark, to arachnophobia, fears take on various forms and hinder our progress. I mean, there is such a thing as ombrophobia, which is the fear of rain, of all things! Personally, I just open the windows, grab a mug of coffee, and enjoy the moment. The gloom of the weather creates a calming, cozy moment for me, rather than stirring up feelings of dread, inconvenience, melancholy, or boredom. However, I do have fears of my own so I'm not judging anyone who is afraid of things that might not make sense to me.

Typically, fear is a good thing. It's a natural response of the body's fight-or-flight mechanism in reaction to a threat in the environment. It allows us to become more focused and more cautious. We are able to analyze our environment better so that we can deal with the threat. However, sometimes humans can adopt excessive or irrational fear of a certain object or a situation. These phobias cripple our normal lives and can cause great distress to us. According to Katherina K. Hauner from the University Feinberg School of Medicine (Watts), such phobias are 'maladaptive responses.' In other words, they stop you from adapting to certain situations.

While we can look at a plethora of fears, there are primarily 10 common ones that hold people back from accepting change in their lives. While I have discussed some of them in the previous chapter, I would like to delve deeper into them in this one, hoping to gain some degree of clarity and help you understand what lies underneath all those thoughts and ideas in your head. After all, they do say that it's best to nip the problem in the bud. The problem is, how can you do that if you don't recognize what the bud really is?

Change

I know what you're thinking; why is the fear of change, well, change itself? But there is a reason for including this.

Welcome to the world of metathesiophobia, which is the fear of change. Yes, that is a real thing.

A lot of people face anxiety when they realize that they are going to experience an uncertain situation. When they realize that a change is looming over the horizon, their fears become constant. They are always worried about what's going to happen, replaying scenarios in their heads, always imagining the worst case scenarios. Their minds are filled with negative ideas, which just adds to their fears.

Now, if it was merely a little fear that you can easily overcome, I wouldn't dedicate a separate section for it. However, it has been shown that certain fears can become so crippling that they can eventually manifest themselves into anxiety disorders and other mental problems (National Alliance on Mental Illness).

You are constantly feeling jumpy. Your fight-or-flight instincts are on overdrive, causing you to feel an overwhelming degree of stress. You feel easily irritated and your thoughts are ominous. These are just some of the effects of a crippling fear of change.

All of these effects prevent you from actually doing something with your life and accomplishing something.

A one-time acquaintance of mine was so afraid of the new location that his job placed him in, that he started to become withdrawn. He would avoid his friends and family, and instead settle down in his apartment with his depression as company. Often, we would try to reach out to him, but would only be met with half-hearted responses and reactions. His work began to suffer too, as his mental state trickled into his performance. It was only when we had to intervene in his life that he realized the harm he was causing himself.

When people try to avoid change, they are merely delaying the inevitable. Their best course of action is to actually plan ahead and strategize their next steps. We're going to look at how to make a stand against the fear of change in Chapter 4. For now, let's look at the next fear.

Loneliness

A friend of mine named Adrian once had to travel to another country for a project. At first, it was an exciting prospect; he was going to meet new people and experience new things. It almost felt like a vacation of sorts, except that he would be mostly occupied with work and might not have a lot of time to spend for himself. The city he had traveled to was Bali, a rather popular tourist destination in the East.

Initially, it was a great experience for Adrian. He got to see wondrous new sights and experience new things that filled him with a sense of adventure.

However, after the initial honeymoon phase with Bali ended, the loneliness began to creep in. He began to miss the weekend barbeques with his friends, the time he spent with his niece and nephew, and the little things that he was used to back home. Despite the fact that he had neighbors, friends, and even a daily routine, it didn't fill him with happiness. He would often feel as though he were missing something; and he would often think of returning home, even at the risk of abandoning the project.

The situation that Adrian faced is not uncommon. Change causes you to embark on a journey where you might not be with the people you once knew. You might have to make decisions that could create distance between you and those that you care about.

Of course, loneliness is not a simple problem that you can just deal with by watching your favorite movie and munching on some snacks. According to the American Psychological Association, loneliness and social isolation can lead to a host of physical and mental problems, including poor sleep, poor cardiovascular function, decreased cognitive abilities, and even depression (Novotney 2019).

In order to avoid potential loneliness, people tend to avoid change itself. They are unsure of where they might end up or how many people they might be forced to stay far away from. It's an uncomfortable thought. Think about it; you now have to adjust to something new while not having the comfort of relying on the company of people you know. That may not be something you can easily get over. Even if you do manage to combat the negative feelings initially, you might start experiencing the effects of loneliness eventually.

Failure

Atychiphobia.

Yes, that is what the fear of failure is called (Marcin 2018).

What's surprising is that the fear of failure is classified as a medical condition. Just to be clear, everyone has a fear of failure. I haven't met anyone who has said to me that they enjoyed failing in their life. No matter what your goals are, you want to make them come true. You're not satisfied if you don't win, since that would mean that you haven't accomplished anything, taken the next step, or gotten what you want. This is especially true when you have a certain purpose in life that you would like to bring into reality.

However, did you know that, as with all phobias, atychiphobia can actually cause physical symptoms as well? An increase in your heart rate, difficulty breathing, sweating, and even tightness in your chest are all indicative of this stress you put on yourself. You may not always experience all of the symptoms, but you might feel at least one of them. When that happens, you become paralyzed.

In some cases, you may experience what is known as analysis paralysis (Taibbi 2019). This is a psychological phenomenon in which you begin to overanalyze so much that it prevents you from making a decision easily. For example, let's say that you have to send a really important email, but you're worried that things might not go your way. You might fail and then have to face the repercussions of the results. This thought makes you analyze the email in minute detail. You may read through the email once, then read it again, and then perhaps read it again. Each time, you feel as though you missed something. Even when the email looks perfect, you can't help but ask yourself questions. When you look at the time, you notice that you have spent nearly half an hour worrying about one single email, when it was probably fine the way it was the first time.

The reality of the situation is that change involves a certain degree of risk. But the fear of failure should not prevent you from accepting the change. You shouldn't be rooted to the spot, constantly worrying about what to do next, since that is far worse than actually dealing with the change.

Rejection

When I mention the word rejection, people often think about relationships. Someone got rejected by the person they love or a partner that they care about.

However, that's not only what rejection is about. The fear of rejection also occurs when it comes to one's needs. For example, let's say that you have been meaning to ask for something from your parents, friends, partner, boss, or anyone else in your life. But you're worried about the fact that they might reject your request. The fear of their rejection will then force you to bottle up your needs. You might even tend to avoid confrontations because you become afraid of speaking out for yourself.

Jacob was a loving father of two who was always worried about asking his wife for some time off for himself during the weekends. She usually tended to reject his requests; and because he was afraid that she would not allow him to spend some with himself—and more specifically, with his friends—he would keep his needs to himself. This was not a healthy decision to make, since it eventually began to lower his morale and cause him undue stress. Eventually, he had a conversation with his wife, and she realized that he needed time to spend on the things he liked doing.

When you fear rejection, you begin to avoid taking care of your own needs. You ignore what you want because you feel either that you might be a burden on someone or that you are not deserving of such needs. This is merely a result of your fear of rejection.

Uncertainty

The harsh reality is that uncertainty surrounds us all. Whether it's the economy, your future, health, or many of the other situations that we worry about, uncertainty is always present in every aspect of our life.

The question is, what do you do about it?

Every venture that you undertake brings its own set of risks. Want to start your own business? Then you have financial and competitor risks. Would you like to take a sabbatical from work? Then you are worried about whether your job is going to be secure upon your return. How about investing in a new house? It could put you in a lot of debt in the future. No matter what decision you make, there will always be a certain degree of risk. Sure, sometimes the risks might be minor enough to ignore them entirely, but that doesn't mean they don't exist at all.

Science has proven that human beings fear the unknown (Carleton 2016). There are numerous reasons for this, including the lack of control they feel, the degree of failure they might experience, the helplessness against a force that they cannot comprehend or explain, among other reasons. Typically, the unknown signifies a change. It will either empower people to plan better and find new courses of action, or it might stop them from progressing further.

Regardless of the results, the fear that claims people's minds when they have to face an unknown obstacle, or a known obstacle with little information, can be overwhelming.

Calamity

Calamities are major incidents that can change the course of our lives, typically for the worse.

When we talk about calamities, we often think of tornados, tsunamis, giant invading spaceships that are here to wipe out entire cities, or the coming of the apocalypse. However, calamities don't have to be on such a large scale.

Perhaps the Merriam-Webster dictionary has the best definition of calamity when it says that it refers to a disastrous event that could lead to great loss or suffering (Merriam-Webster, "Definition of CALAMITY"). Such events don't have to be connected to nature or other large entities. They can occur on a personal scale – the death of a family member, a crippling injury, a debilitating disease, a major financial shutdown of the economy – all create personal calamities that can drastically change your life. Such calamities often depict a change on an extreme level.

For example, a financial crash leads to loss of jobs. If you happen to be one of those people who got laid off, then there is no way for you to keep your house and its mortgage payments.

You might be forced to sell the house and other assets, eventually transferring to a small apartment. That would be a huge change in your life. Things might become even more frightening when you also have a family to support, knowing that they will all have to adjust to a new life without their previous luxuries.

We always fear such changes. It's for that reason that we hesitate to take risks or try to make plans. For example, we avoid changing jobs because we're afraid that another global economic crash like the one that occurred in 2007-2008 might happen again (Singh 2020), causing widespread damage to many people's jobs and lives.

Our fear increases dramatically if we have survived one calamity in our lives. We often feel as though another one is just around the corner, and it's just a matter of time before we face it. But we would rather avoid it or prevent it from happening again by taking certain steps. Such thoughts force us to hunker down in our present situation, even though that may not be what we want. After all, we all have things we would like to accomplish. We might want to be famous, earn a lot of money, become the best parent in the world, find a great job, graduate from university, or get a six-pack so strong that it could deflect a heavyweight boxer's punch.

However, what we fear is calamity – the fact that change could create a disturbance so vast in our lives, that it could only lead to a major disaster.

Pain

When I say pain, I don't mean physical pain. I'm referring to psychological or emotional pain that can cause you to become fearful of changes in the future.

Although, now that we're on the topic of physical and emotional reactions, perhaps we could also talk about the connection between the two.

While research on the subject is still being carried out, it has been shown that emotional pain can actually have physical effects as well (Abdallah and Geha 2017). In some cases, the pain can lead to physical discomfort rather than pain. But the point remains; whether you experience just emotional pain or it leads to physical effects as well, none of us actually enjoy the experience. The point is, you must take care of your mental and emotional health, as too much distress or anguish can reflect poorly on your body through problems like migraines or headaches, nausea, stomach ulcers, chest pain, back pain, and muscle tension. These may seem like minor irritants, but when experienced frequently enough – or to an intense degree – they can have more serious and debilitating consequences down the road if they're not managed properly.

We avoid the emotional distress certain situations cause us. We might have felt such pain in the past; after all, we know as children what it feels like to be sad, disappointed, hurt, or offended. All of these emotional states present their own degree of pain, but they are pain nevertheless. For example, disappointment may not present a feeling that is stronger than, say, a tragedy. Despite that, no one would be okay with disappointments and the emotional toll it can take on their minds.

Pain is an important reaction, whether mental or physical. It helps us avoid damage and reminds us of our limitations. However, when it starts to take over your mind and prevents you from making progress, then it begins to work against you.

Judgment

People are capable of going to extreme lengths to ensure that they are perceived in a certain light by others. They might hide their true feelings or needs from their partners or friends.

We all want to look good in front of others, and we want to be liked by others. This does not lead merely to a personal benefit but provides other advantages as well. When you are perceived positively by others, you have more company. This eventually leads you to make more friends, better connections or even access to more sources of help.

This idea of being part of a community is a leftover mechanism from our ancestors. Rather than looking to psychology to explain this phenomenon, perhaps we might need to look into history, for that's where the answers lie. What better way to examine our past than to seek our answers from the renowned Smithsonian National Museum of Natural History? According to the Smithsonian, ancient humans would join a group or a tribe because it was essential for their survival. You might recognize the phrase "strength in numbers." It's exactly as the phrase means; if you were living in a cave with nothing but animal skin to cover your privates, then you had better not be living alone because that might mean that you would be the hors d'oeuvre on the tiger's next menu.

The need to be part of a social group or a 'tribe' still persists to this day, although our social needs have developed to satisfy not just our survival needs (unless there are tigers roaming around your city block), but also our emotional demands.

We want to love and feel loved in return. Remember what we said about our emotional reactions? They are mainly managed by our subconscious mind. The more emotions we feed it, then the more it stores them in our memory for future use.

What do you think happens when you keep telling your subconscious mind that you crave the company of others? It sends you ideas to do everything you can to avoid being lonely. You begin to rely on the judgment of others because you want to be part of the group. You fear the fact that your friends or acquaintances might abandon you if they don't like what you are.

The reality is that everything you need to believe is right within you. It's just not easy convincing a part of your brain that has been conditioned to think otherwise.

Inadequacy

As adults, we have the power to reason against certain ideas or beliefs. But as children we don't necessarily have the required level of experience and wisdom to explain everything that happens to us.

I bring up childhood because that is when feelings of inadequacy develop the most. That's not to say that we can't start experiencing low self-esteem, shame, and even powerlessness as adults, but it creates the biggest impact when we are young and our brains are still trying to grasp various ideas about the world around us.

Regardless of when you start feeling inadequate, the results are often terrifying. Parents start feeling inadequate when they realize that they may not be providing enough for their children. Workplace bullying or harassment lowers the self-confidence and value people hold about themselves. You might also begin to experience feelings of inadequacy because of the way ideas are presented in the media. Currently, we have certain expectations for beauty, wealth, power, physical fitness, or fame. All of these ideas twist our perception of our world and can make us feel as though we don't have a lot of value in society.

We then start to carefully create a life that revolves around trying to attain a certain standard or level of quality. We don't focus on goals because they hold purpose to us. Rather, we choose to pick up goals that help us improve our self-worth. While there's nothing wrong with that in and of itself, it does affect your growth and progress if you start focusing on it too much. You begin to ignore your goals and other ideas that you might have previously thought of.

More importantly, you begin to fear change. After all, even the slightest change might feel like a threat to you. You don't want anything to disrupt the life you have worked hard to create around your standards.

Our focus should be on our own strengths and successes, because when we truly begin to look inwards, we realize that we are more capable and stronger than we give ourselves credit for.

Freedom

Finally, let's look at the concept of freedom. More specifically, the loss of it.

When change occurs, we might gain something, and we might lose something as well. One of the factors that we fear losing is the freedom we enjoy. When I say freedom, I'm not talking about the ability to do whatever you want.

Here's an example. Let's say that you've been working in an office that's close to your home. Because of the distance, you are able to travel to your workplace using a bicycle. This also allows you to catch some extra sleep in the morning. Imagine that you got accepted to work in a better job with a better salary and great colleagues. The only difference is that you might have to travel a little – not too much, but it would require a short walk and a shorter subway trip – to reach your office. You definitely enjoyed the freedom you had before when you could just decide to wake up late if you liked. But does that mean you won't shift to a better job just because you are worried about losing that small freedom?

For a lot of people, that decision is quite difficult to make. They end up becoming paralyzed by fear because they begin to overthink about their situation. They believe that the loss of freedom means that something terrible is about to happen. Unable to weigh the pros and cons in order to make an informed decision, all they see are the worst aspects of the change.

Fear Street

One of the important features of the fears that we have just examined is that they don't happen individually. This means that you don't just face the fear of inadequacy on its own, but rather different kinds of fears often overlap. You might have to face multiple fears which become challenging to deal with all at once.

Different changes bring their own cocktail of fears into your life. For example, the changes that age brings lead to a fear of growing old. This creates **uncertainty** about the future, especially if we haven't managed to achieve our life's purpose or our goals. At the same time, we can worry about the **loneliness** we might experience in the future. Will my family still be around? How many friends will I have left in my old age? Will my partner leave the mortal plane before me? Also, let's not forget the loss of **freedom** people fear they might experience. After all, old age means that people may not have the same physical and mental capabilities compared to their younger selves. So what will their life be like at that point? Will they still have the freedom to engage in physical activities or take part in their hobbies? Will they have enough mobility to partake in simple, everyday tasks and take care of themselves?

Let's talk about another fear; the fear of marriage. Accepting to live the rest of your life with someone is a big change. Most people fear that they might lose the **freedom** that they once enjoyed when they were single. After all, they won't be able to just step out of the house whenever they feel like it and spend time away for as long as they want without letting their partner know what's going on or when they'll be back. People might also fear being inadequate. Are they good enough for their partner? Are they strong enough to take on responsibilities they might share? Do they have the courage to ensure the relationship is long-lasting? People might also worry about the **pain** they might endure. They imagine that certain situations might cause lasting emotional pain and that may not be something they are ready to face. More importantly, they are worried that there might be a day when their partners might **reject** them.

Think about the various changes people fear, from relationships to moving to a new location to even following their goals. Each of these changes will have a host of fears that cripple people into inactivity.

Hindsight 20/20

I was doing so many things wrong in my life. I just did not want to admit it.

Perhaps I didn't even want to think of the fact that I was doing something wrong. After all, I would trudge through the day and at the end of it, I would try to numb all the stress, frustrations, and other negative emotions I was feeling by watching a movie, hanging out with my friends, or just reading a book. In short, I would pretend to be okay.

Hey, at least I was doing something, right?

That was my justification for anything that would go wrong; that I was at least being productive, even though I probably would not have been able to explain exactly what productivity looked like.

I suppose looking back, I could easily plot my experiences into 5 major areas of focus.

One

I had all but lost my sense of self. I had no idea how it happened, but gradually, everything started to come to a pause as I began to resist even the smallest of changes in my life.

I became a passive observer, not an active instigator, and I turned into someone who preferred to watch things happen instead of trying to do something to progress my life. Looking back to that time, it's safe to say that I wasn't brave enough to plough through. It felt as though I didn't have it in me to take control of my life all on my own. Yet, I had little patience whenever I felt I was losing control, even though I had no intention of doing something constructive about it.

It was as though I was content with losing things, but I would do nothing to gain something. A small portion of me still wanted to hit back at life, but I kept myself from taking the necessary steps. I could tackle this constant doubt, but I had no courage—and that is something I needed the most, something that I had to build on my own.

I remember the time where I had finally taken a two-week vacation from my work. I truly wanted to travel somewhere exotic. I had thought about Thailand, Turkey, Japan, Ireland, or a place with a lot of nature. After all, I was a city boy, and I needed some sense of adventure in my life.

What happened?

Well, in the end I just decided to stay at home. All the years of passivity had diminished my sense of wonder and curiosity. I was not willing to take risks because I had never experienced what it was like to take them.

Video games, sleeping, taking a small walk outside, sleeping, ordering food from outside, sleeping, spending time with friends, and did I mention sleeping? That was what my vacation boiled down to, all because I was so afraid of actually making a bold decision on my own.

Two

Remember the thing about losing control? I was not ready to give up on some of the things that gave me a sense of control.

When you plan to build your own job – going independent, that is – you start feeling that things might not be stable, and could spiral out. When doing freelance work, you are, for the most part, your own boss and have the responsibility of making all executive and creative decisions. Nearly all outcomes and facets of your job depend on you alone. The organizations that people work for provide a ceiling over your head. They provide a culture and don't really leave much of the decision-making process to you, unless you're part of the highest levels of management. This makes you feel safe. Since you are not the one making decisions, you get used to low-risk scenarios. At the same time, it also gives you a sense of control over small things. Fear of losing that control simply drove home the point that I was unworthy of taking actions and seeing them through.

What do I mean by that? Well, as long as you have a set of tasks such as checking your emails, adding notes to a document, or doing something repeatedly with mild variations, you don't take creative risks. When that happens, you begin to get used to repetitions. Why do something unique when you can do the same and get paid for it at the end of the day?

Even in that situation, I wanted to feel as though I was doing something valuable. I had become rigid with my self-image, trying to force a narrative that I was still relevant, even when I wasn't.

After all, we don't like to admit to ourselves that there might be something wrong with our lives. That maybe we need to change something because what we're doing is just not making us happy.

Three

Because I wasn't ready to accept who I was, I started drifting away from what mattered. The negative thoughts and narratives would drive me to anger and frustration.

Rather than deal with those frustrations, I began to justify them. If I were to commit mistakes in the office, fail in standing on my own two legs, not take care of the family, or not be there for those loved ones who needed me the most, what good was I? I had to just keep going, keep doing what I was doing. That was the only way.

It wasn't, of course, but that's what I had trained my mind to believe.

I wasn't taking risks, and that was detrimental to my progress.

What was the result of that? It's often easy, in such cases, to play the blame game. But it only makes you petty, as it did to me. Because I wasn't ready to acknowledge my flaws, I was not going to accept that I was the reason behind getting myself stuck in life. This is a phenomenon that psychologists have noticed in people who are not willing to change the undesirable aspects of their life; they begin to play the blame game (Warren 2014).

Four

The cycle repeated because I'd give in to my negative thoughts instead of challenging them. As a result, I was trapped in anxiety, panic attacks, and a constant, nagging self-doubt.

You can see how this was the root of the problem right from the beginning. The first seed of doubt takes over, and you start doubting who you are. This feeds your ego because, again, you don't want to be confronted with a changing self—a constant tug of war.

However, there was nothing I could do about it. All I did was shift my locus of control.

What is that, you ask? Well, to understand this, we need to look at why successful people are able to be the accomplished individuals they are. What separates them from those who are unsuccessful or just average? Is it their work ethic? Is it the fact that they wake up early in the morning? Could it be their attention to a healthy diet and good sleep?

While all of those factors are important, there is really one primary trait that separates those who are successful from those who are not. Well, two, if you include the idea that successful people welcome change into their lives.

I'm talking about locus of control. According to the American Psychological Association, the locus of control refers to the degree to which people are able to take responsibility for the events and situations in their life as opposed to blaming external forces (American Psychological Association).

Successful people have an internal locus of control. This means that they like to believe that they are in control of their lives. If something goes wrong, then it is up to them to discover a solution.

On the other hand, unsuccessful people have an external locus of control. Rather than take responsibility for their lives, they choose to blame external forces for their misfortunes.

Just to be clear, there isn't anything wrong with blaming an external event or stimulus. Sometimes, such claims can be true. A change in economy can definitely affect your business. A global situation that forces countries to implement lockdown laws can definitely impact your life routines.

However, one's default reaction should not be to blame such incidents. Successful people feel the effects of unpredictable situations. But the difference in their approach is that they are already thinking of what to do next. They are forming ideas about how to counter the bad luck that they have been dealt. You see, it isn't really about *what* happens, necessarily, but how you *react* to it.

As you might have guessed, I was someone who preferred to approach my life with an internal locus of control.

Five

The final nail in the coffin was my inability to move out of this stagnated state I had driven myself into. I'd get rays of hope once in a while but would never take action, pushing all the hard work of creating a motivational platform to the next day, which – admittedly – never comes.

After all, we always like to delay things to the future – that magical place where all our goals and actions come true. When we think of the future, we like to imagine an indefinite period of time; and we overestimate the time that is available to us.

In other words, we begin to procrastinate. According to an article published in the American Psychological Association, procrastination is the act of delaying tasks to a future date (Ferrari 2010). Apart from making us unproductive, procrastination also turns us into poor time estimators. We often think that we have enough time to complete our projects, tasks, ideas, or chores in the future. But we usually don't. We don't make accurate estimations, we make optimistic ones. After all, if we realized we didn't have any time, we wouldn't try to delay our work or progress, now would we?

Eventually, it was this lethargic approach to my life that my friends and family began to observe in me. When they realized that I needed help, they had a major intervention (well, several of them, to be honest). Each time they talked to me, it was as though they were holding a mirror to my face and asking me to look at the person reflected back.

Was I proud of that person? Absolutely not.

They made me realize that my fear of change was a result of my lack of initiative. Because I was always willing to accept my situation without questioning it, I had slowly begun to develop a fear of change and almost a numbness to it.

When I realized my mistake, I decided to fight back. The result was the set of steps that I am about to share with you.

4

Make the CHANGE Against Fear of Change

What do we do when we have a fear of change? Well, we can simply change it.

Yes, I know that's an odd statement to make, but you will understand it completely by the time you reach the end of this chapter.

Based on my experiences, I have created a 6-step program that can help you fight your fear of change and be ready to tackle new situations and ideas.

Step 1: Courage

I would like to start this step by saying that courage has got nothing to do with being fearless; rather, it's the ability to charge at your fears, not exactly without thinking, but in a manner where you cast away any excuses you have to stall, and instead you just *do*. Just take a step. Just take action and make a tangible change, however miniscule. In fact, you can think of courage as the strength and resilience you have when you are faced with challenges, pain, tragedies, or misfortunes. If you would truly like to make changes, then you need to develop the courage within yourself. Not only does it help build your resilience, but it also improves your confidence.

But how can one build courage? Is there a magic potion that can instantly unlock your bravery, like those video games that allow you to upgrade your skills?

Not really. However, don't be disappointed, because there is a way for you to boost your courage.

Exercise #1: Courage Under Fire

1. Identify Your Fears

Every fear has a name; you simply have to find it. If you are not able to recognize what you're afraid of, your fear is going to be an unknown entity. That is a frightening idea, since human beings are naturally afraid of the unknown. This becomes a tricky situation because you begin to fear the fear itself.

I want you to start making a note of your goals. List down everything you would like to do. Use a notebook, a piece of paper, or even a note-taking app on your device. Once you have listed your goals, focus on the most important one.

Start listing down all the reasons you are unable to make progress on your goal.

Here's an example.

Goal: I would like to start my own business.

Challenges/Potential Obstacles:

- I feel as though it will be expensive.
- I'm worried that things won't go my way and I will end up with a big loss.
- People are not going to like what I have to offer.

Remember, the challenges should include all the ideas that you fear.

2. *Create Solutions*

Start thinking of solutions to combat your fears. You don't have to necessarily think of them all by yourself; you can conduct research on the internet or seek out help from your friends.

The main strategy in this step is to actually discover actionable solutions.

Looking back at the goal I had listed in my previous step, which was to start my own business, I would probably list down solutions such as the following:

- Try to create a business plan.
- Start small. No need to invest heavily and create big risks.
- Check out the market and see what I can discover.

3. *Start Writing Down Solutions to Your Fears*

After a while, you will get used to the idea of finding solutions for the challenges you face in your life. Now start focusing directly on your fears. For example, let's say that you have a fear of public spaces.

Once your fear has been identified, list down solutions with which you can try to combat the fear in question. It's okay to take slow steps. Taking the example of the fear of public places, then maybe your first step is to engage with your neighbors or maybe you feel comfortable having a conversation with the local cafe barista. Maybe you could try sitting on a park bench and just people-watch, immersing yourself in an environment where there *is* public activity around you, but your engagement is minimal. Make simple changes that can allow you to break out of your shell slowly.

4. Action Speaks Louder

Once you have written down your solutions, act upon them. Bonus points for focusing on the solutions on a regular basis and practicing them consistently! The more you become acclimated to your fears and solutions, the more you are able to slowly overcome them.

Step 2: Humility

As you begin to work on your courage, you will slowly begin to discover not just your fears, but your flaws and weaknesses as well.

Many people, when confronted with their shortcomings, go into denial mode. However, that only helps support your fears and restrict the degree of courage you can attain. You need to understand that every single person on the planet has flaws. However, not everyone has the courage to accept them. The ability to accept those flaws will help you develop a realistic outlook towards life, which brings us to the next exercise.

Exercise #2: Flawless Victory

Every time you discover a fear and take action to solve it, make another list to record the flaws about yourself that you come across.

Once you have done so, go through each flaw and then ask the following questions to gain better perspective about them and what your next course of action should be:

- Why does this flaw make me view myself in a negative light?
- Am I seeing this flaw because I'm comparing myself to someone else?
- Is it really that bad that I have this flaw?
- Going further, is this so-called 'flaw' something I have control over, or is it something I can't change?
- If so, would I like to do something about it? If so, how can I overcome it?
- Is it important to deal with it to achieve my long-term goals?

Here's an example. Let's say that you're planning to head to the gym and gain a fit body. However, you're slightly shorter than the average person, and you think of this as a flaw. Use the above questions to understand whether being fairly short has any real impact on your fitness goals. If it doesn't affect your progress towards six-pack abs, then do you really have to worry about it?

Previously, when you were thinking about your flaws, you were in a pessimistic state. Now, instead of going the opposite route towards unrealistic optimism – and perhaps clinging to a hope for a change that will never come – humility will help you understand where you are lacking, accept those flaws, and then work in conjunction with them to create realistic, tangible plans for your goals.

Don't forget to give some love to yourself as well. Being a realist doesn't have to equate to hating on yourself. Self-love and compassion go a long way in encouraging your inner-self and to keep yourself motivated. You are, after all, trying your best, and the cognizance or realization that you have a flaw coupled with your willingness to improve already puts you one step ahead.

Step 3: Accountability

Once you have started to work on your humility, you will then focus on your locus of control. Remember what I had mentioned about the difference between successful and unsuccessful people? Well, you're now going to transform yourself into a person who feels successful.

In order to do that, you need to develop your sense of accountability. But that's easier said than done, of course. It almost seems like asking someone without any knowledge of vehicle engineering to build an electrical car; that's not going to happen. However, developing accountability does not have to be such a daunting endeavor. In fact, all you need is a powerful technique.

Exercise #3: With Great Power Comes Great Responsibility

Once again, for this exercise you are going to write down your goals. You can also make use of the list you created before.

This time, you are going to list all the points that you think are reasons why you haven't accomplished your goals or made much progress in them. Your reasons can be anything; you did not have sufficient financial funds, the laws changed abruptly, the weather was bad, your Chinese zodiac sign mentioned that this was the year of misfortune, or you think Cthulhu has cursed you. It doesn't matter. Just record your reasons without judgment or blame.

Once you have written down the reasons, group them into two sections. One section should contain all the reasons that are a result of your actions. The other section will list all the reasons that occurred due to external forces.

Focus on the external forces first. Think about what you can do in order to deal with them, protect against them, or have a 'Plan B' in case they happen. After you have gone through the external forces, turn your attention to the internal forces list, which features personal reasons that have prevented you from achieving your goals. Try to think of solutions or ideas to deal with them, and write them down.

After creating all the solutions, you are then going to take the most important step. You are going to make a note of this statement:

Whatever happens from now on is my responsibility.

From this point onwards, you are going to focus on the solutions to the problem rather than the problem itself. More importantly, you are going to work on those solutions with the idea that your actions alone are responsible for the degree of success you attain with them. Sure, there might be unexpected scenarios that might appear suddenly. If they do, then you are going to have to evaluate them and think of the next steps.

This exercise will train you to avoid becoming frozen with indecision and automatically resort to the blame game. Instead, it will force you to take responsibility for your actions, thereby making you accountable for your goals.

Step 4: Negativity

While courage and confidence will keep you focused, you will have to face the inner demons and come out of your cycle of self-doubt. Negativity is that inner demon. But it's not just any demon; it's one that is always hungry.

It eats at your joy, consumes your optimism, and makes your reality feel all black and white.

Your courage, humility, and accountability are only going to get you so far. Because eventually it becomes a battle of attrition. The more you experience negativity, the more your self-esteem and confidence begin to wear down. Eventually, your self-belief will suffer a death by a thousand cuts of negativity.

Before that can happen, let's see what you can do about it.

Exercise #4: Full Stop

This is a simple exercise that you can practice anywhere. The more you use it, the more you will begin to feel aware of your thoughts. This process will help you to stop the influx of negative thoughts before they can take over your mind and wreak havoc in your head.

Whenever you plan something and experience negative thoughts permeating your consciousness, stop thinking. Focus on the negative thoughts. Ask yourself these questions:

- Why do I have these thoughts? Do they have anything valuable to contribute?
- Are they warning me about something or are they simply a result of my fears?
- I know that every endeavor possesses a certain degree of challenge. Does that mean that I should listen to the negative thoughts I am having right now?
- What can I say to answer these thoughts?

The more you become aware of your thoughts and begin to question them, the more they become hesitant to intrude on your musings. Your subconscious gets the message; it learns to take a hint and shut up, which is probably what you want in a lot of situations.

Step 5: Growth

Growth also means that you evolve into a better self, one that helps you leave a better impact around you, inspiring others to take greater strides while you continue to wear your courage and confidence on your sleeve. Most people think of growth as a complete transformation, but that's not always the case. When you experience growth, you take your existing knowledge, skills, and experience and give it an update. Sometimes, you might have to let go of existing beliefs. Other times, you might have to give up on skills that are outdated.

But in the end, you are usually trading a part of what you have for something that is better, more accurate, or more relevant. Therefore, growth might not always be this fantastical epiphany where you do this and that and suddenly everything is perfect. Growth is a culmination of slow, gradual steps that you take day-to-day. You also might not feel progress as you move along, but when you look back at the work you've done overall you'll realize just how far you've come.

Growth may seem like an easy concept to grasp, but it actually requires considerable practice to truly master. Which is why we have the following exercise.

Exercise #5: Growing Pains

There are three areas that you need to focus on that will help you grow.

The first is your belief system. One of the most prevalent biases that apply to our lives today is confirmation bias. According to psychologists (Nickerson 1998), confirmation bias is a phenomenon that means people look for information, ideas, or theories that support their preexisting beliefs and avoid anything that might even remotely contradict them. This eventually becomes a serious flaw in character because you might end up believing that you're always right. In order to arrive at the best conclusion, make sure that you are viewing two sides of an argument before you can rationally – and with all the right information – decide what is truly right, moral, or ethical. It doesn't matter how difficult it may be to listen to opposing views. For example, if you come across a flat-earther, then don't just dismiss their claims. This doesn't mean you are agreeing with them. Rather, you're listening to their viewpoints, facts, and ideas before coming to a conclusion. After all, if I ask you how you can effectively prove a flat-earther wrong without resorting to ad hominems or emotions, then it might be a fairly difficult job.

The next area focuses on your skills. No matter how good you think you are, always look for ways to improve yourself. Look for challenges. Find new ways to approach a problem. For example, let's say that you feel as though you are a good writer, then try to challenge yourself to approach topics that you never would have before. Or, aside from topics, challenge yourself to write in a different medium or learn how to write using a different platform or computer program. Looking at the rate of technological and other innovations, one's skill could become outdated if it does not match the requirements of the time. Don't lose any opportunities to become better.

The final area you need to focus on is your memory. However, in this case, you won't be trying to grow your memory, but to grow *out* of it. What do I mean? I would like you to forgive yourself for your past mistakes and make peace with the things that have already happened. You won't be needing them where you're going. Don't worry about the embarrassing situations you have faced or the opportunities you have lost. They are not going to come back, so there is no point in thinking about them. Focus on what you have now and how you can improve in the future.

Step 6: Ego

With growth comes an increasing frequency of your ego's presence. You can try to avoid it for a while, but you will have to face it eventually.

Just to be clear, there is nothing wrong with being proud of yourself, your loved ones, or even your ideas and accomplishments. However, things take a turn for the worst if you start developing excessive pride. You will begin to consider yourself superior to others and that you're always right. You won't give yourself room to grow or become a better person because you think there's nothing that needs changing.

Remember: a growing plant cannot be contained in a small pot; it needs a new house constantly. In the same way, you cannot expect to be the same forever. When you break your old habits, challenge your ego, and find ways to become a better version of yourself, you will naturally outgrow what once served you.

Of course, the grand question is this: just how do you deal with your ego?

Exercise #6: Pride and Prejudice

The best method for ensuring that you are keeping your ego under check is to question it every time you become aware of its influence. For example, let's say that you're having a conversation with a friend and they point out a fault that you have. Don't immediately become defensive. You can instead let your friend know that you will think about what they have said. When you get the time later, reflect on your friend's words and ask yourself; was my friend right? Should I accept this feedback or were they actually really offensive about it? How can I respond to them now?

If you feel as though your friend was wrong about you, then the best way to approach the situation is to take your ego out of the equation. Let them know that what they told you offended you, but try not to be too emotional about it. Don't corner them; but rather try to understand where they were coming from in their criticism.

In a similar manner, find out ways you can deal with a situation without using your ego. Question it. Find out why you feel a certain way. Even if their assessment is wrong, always remain vigilant about areas you can improve and stay humble. Never get so comfortable with yourself that you refuse to see where you might be the bad guy.

Now that we understand the six main areas you have to focus on, I would like to revisit one particular area in more detail.

I'm talking about courage.

5

When Facing Change, Courage Is Your Best Friend

We all come across various obstacles or challenges in our lives. We face tragedies. We experience pain, both physical and psychological. We stumble our way through this grand experience we call life.

Some of us just decide to give up, allowing life to carry them wherever it takes them. Others fight against the current. They know that once they have crossed the worst part, they will arrive at a destination that is better than what they have now.

When we talk about Arthurian legends, we often mention King Arthur, Lady of the Lake, and Excalibur. We're familiar with these names because pop culture has used them in various ways over the years. In fact, you might even know of Merlin and Lancelot.

But how about if I throw you the name Gawain?

Unless you're already familiar with Arthurian legends, you would probably be asking, *who?* That, or you might have gone to Google to search the name and now claim that you know who that is (I know your tricks because I would probably have done the same to save face).

The story of Sir Gawain is probably the most fascinating to me. In the legends, Sir Gawain might just be the greatest knight among King Arthur's ensemble. One tale talks about the Green Knight, a mysterious figure who approaches King Arthur and then challenges him to a duel. Despite having a fear of death, Sir Gawain stands up to face the knight. After beheading the knight, Sir Gawain believes that he has won the duel. But that's not the case. The Green Knight rises and then informs Gawain that he must appear before the knight in the following year so that he, too, can be beheaded. That's the rule of the deal.

Despite knowing his fate, Sir Gawain courageously marches forward. He knows that if he declines, then the knight might come for King Arthur. The further he travels on his journey, the more his fear grows. But nevertheless, he marches on ever so closer to his anticipated demise.

Eventually, the Green Knight reveals that all of this was a test to see the loyalty and courage that Sir Gawain possessed, and he is then rewarded for keeping his promise.

I'm not saying that you need to find someone that threatens to behead you. That's absurd. However, we all have our own version of the Green Knight.

It could be our daily habits that confine us to a life of regression and disappointments. It could be our lack of goals that make us feel as though we're not destined to accomplish anything. It could also be our high levels of procrastination. There are many reasons why we feel as though we're not capable of growing.

All of the above situations bring with them fears and obstacles. These are challenges that we try to avoid completely. Changing daily habits means that we have to face the unknown. Trying to discover new goals means that we have to start facing ourselves. Combating procrastination means that we have to actively step out of our comfort zones. All of these are our Green Knights.

They are situations, events, or experiences that force us to confront a threat that we are not usually accustomed to. After all, if we were used to something, then it wouldn't necessarily be called a threat, now would it?

Real life is a succession of battles. You might think that when you're doing nothing – such as when you're procrastinating – then you aren't actually fighting a battle. But you are. Your mind is hosting a duel where action is on one corner of the ring and inaction is on the other.

During such battles, those small doses of courage help keep us on track and allow us to take on things that might be seemingly insurmountable.

Think back to your early days, to experiences with which a little courage helped you to achieve things which have now become mundane. Take cycling, for example. The risk of accidentally falling off or running into an obstacle never left, but you were courageous and bold, even as a child, to take on those challenges.

As you grew up, your experiences softened you. They made you hesitant.

According to Robert L. Leahy, the Director of The American Institute for Cognitive Therapy (Leahy 2008), some of our fears have been learned while others we are born into.

If you think of human beings as hardware, then we are preloaded with certain fears as our software. They come with every copy of the human mind, so you have no choice but to live with them. Since we aren't exactly wise during the first ten years of our lives – and maybe not even the next ten – we have to live with these fears without ever having to deal with them properly.

Now let's combine this discovery of fears with the result of different research that was conducted on the human mind; that we are naturally lazy. As we have seen in the introduction of this book, researchers from Simon Fraser University in Canada discovered that we try to save energy.

This becomes a vicious loop that is self-sustaining. It starts with the fear of something. Maybe it is the commitment towards a partner or the risk of new ventures. Regardless of the situation, you become so afraid that it paralyzes you to the point of indecision. You begin to procrastinate. Rather than taking action, you *think* about taking action. The more you procrastinate, the more you become lazy.

The more lazy you become, the more the power of your fear increases. Where once it was a force that was quite intimidating, it has now metamorphosed into a force that is actually threatening and dangerous. You've been thinking about it for so long that you have turned it into a gigantic beast that cannot be toppled. This in turn makes you procrastinate more. and the cycle continues.

Of course, you don't like to consider yourself lazy, no one does. Humans are capable of explaining a lot of circumstances. We can justify anything to make it look positive because we don't want to be the villains of our own story.

So how do we fight this fear? What can we do to overcome it? After all, courage isn't exactly the absence of fear. It's the actions we take in the presence of fear. Remember that in Chapter 4, we looked at a simple exercise to identify your fears and create appropriate solutions. In this chapter, we are going to delve deeper into fear. Essentially, we are going to take a deeper look at the step "Identify Your Fears" so you know just how you should be able to go about the identification process.

Our first step is to question our fears properly. There are seven vital questions that you can ask your fears:

1. What am I afraid of? Explain this question in as much detail as possible.
2. If I say "yes" to the change, will I be able to follow the kind of life I want to live?
3. Imagine myself three years from now. Will that person regret turning down the change that I received right now? Will that person be happy that I did not take the initiative to do what I wanted to do?
4. Who are the people who are going to either be involved in this change or be affected by it? Am I holding myself back because I'm trying to please someone or worried that I will disappoint them?
5. What new opportunities will I receive if I say 'yes' to this change?
6. What are the different lessons that I could learn from the opportunity I am presented? What skills or experiences can I gain?
7. Perhaps one of the most important questions of all; will the change make me happy, content, and feeling better about myself?

The above questions should help you understand whether the risk you are about to take is worth it or not. After all, not everything you would like to do is beneficial for you. You might have a goal that may not give you a sense of purpose. Asking the above questions will ensure you home in on the goals that truly matter to you.

They will also help you gain more confidence in the things you would like to do.

Speaking of confidence, what's the difference between it and courage?

Merriam-Webster defines courage as the moral and mental strength to endure, resist, and face your fears, challenges or dangers (Merriam-Webster, "Definition of COURAGE"). When you look at the definition of confidence, the dictionary mentions that it is the quality of a person where they are certain about something (Merriam-Webster, "Definition of CONFIDENCE"). When you extend the definition of confidence to self-confidence, then it essentially refers to the quality of a person where they are certain about themselves and their abilities, knowledge, memories, and experiences.

This means that courage is the first step towards progress. After all, you need courage to take a step forward, face your challenges, find a solution, or deal with a threat. However, courage alone cannot sustain you in the long run. In this case, you need to rely on your self-confidence.

Why?

Think about it this way. If you're not sure of yourself or a certain aspect about yourself, then how likely are you to continue the journey you have undertaken? Let's look at an example.

You have been meaning to change your job for a long time. However, you have always felt unsure of your capabilities, and that has prevented you from actively seeking out new employment opportunities. You are just afraid to apply for new job positions.

Eventually, you muster the **courage** to apply for a job. That single action emboldens you to apply for more jobs, increasing your familiarity with the process so it becomes something more easy and routine. Eventually, you receive a call for an interview.

Once again, you garner the necessary courage to head into the interview. It is only when the interview starts that you realize just how nervous you are. At this point, you need the **confidence** to carry yourself properly. You need confidence to present yourself as the person the company should hire.

This situation applies to many areas of your life. Courage only helps you face the challenge, but it is confidence that helps you believe in yourself enough to keep your mind focused on the end goal.

But can you develop confidence? Can you improve it to a point where you can rely on it?

Yes you can!

Exercise #7: Belief in the Self

1. It's a Goal!

The first step you need to take is to evaluate your goals. At this point, you might have performed the exercise where you noted down all your goals. If you haven't done it already, then what are you waiting for?

Once you have made a list of all your goals, you then have to decide which one among them you would like to pursue immediately. I would recommend focusing on one goal at a time so that you are able to give it your full attention.

2. *List of Things*

In this step, you should list all the skills and knowledge necessary to accomplish the goal.

For example, if you would like to prepare delicious food so that you can open your own restaurant, then think about what you need to do to make it happen. You might need to join culinary school, if you're able to. Alternatively, you need to master the dishes, ingredients, and flavors you will be using in your restaurant.

In some cases, you may not require skills, but knowledge. If you would like to be a better software developer or a successful lawyer, then knowledge is the tool that will allow you to succeed.

Regardless of whether you need skills or knowledge, the next step is the same.

3. *Practice Makes Perfect*

Now start practicing. Repeat the steps. Master the skill and improve your knowledge through learning.

Build your experience and make sure that you find ways to implement or express your skills and knowledge. Planning to be a great guitarist? Play what you learn in front of an audience or create your own profile on social media to upload videos and display your skills. Are you studying to become a doctor and you learned something new? Then discuss it with your peers and superiors so you can get their feedback as well.

Don't just stop at the learning process. Use what you know or have in practice. Once you do, keep practicing until you have gained a certain degree of mastery. That's when you stop doubting yourself and become confident in your abilities.

4. *Measure Your Progress*

Every time you make progress, make sure that you're looking back at the progress you have already made. It's easy for us to get caught in the repetitive loop of looking forward to the challenges ahead of us without looking back to admire how far we have come, and what we've already accomplished.

Looking at your progress allows you to look at your growth, which in turn boosts the confidence you feel in yourself.

Even personal skills require the same attention. If you're not confident about speaking publicly, then keep training until you master it. I know that it might sound like a rather simple suggestion, but too often, people don't focus on the basics. They want to try something revolutionary that has the capability to instantly change their lives. The reality is that such changes rarely exist.

If you want to master something, even if that something is confidence in yourself, then you need to keep repeating the basics. There is no shortcut to mastering something new.

The Leader and the Follower

Remember that you need to train your courage first before you can train your confidence.

You might ask me why. That's a valid question.

Think of the relationship between courage and confidence as that of a leader and a follower.

Who is the leader?

It's courage, of course. Courage leads the way for progress. It's the force that breaks barriers and faces the onslaught of oncoming obstacles. You're able to wield courage as your weapon or as your shield.

Confidence is the follower. It's the army that the leader needs to keep making progress. Imagine a battlefield, and the leader is running head-first into enemy territory all by himself. What is he going to gain? He might as well give up and call it a day because he is definitely going to lose. Courage serves more as the initial inspiration, motivation, and taking that first step. But with that, you also need substance to follow through.

Now imagine that the leader has the power of an army behind him. He's definitely going to feel more confident facing the enemy. Moreover, the more well-trained the army is, the more confidence he'll have. In other words, the more you train your skills and knowledge, the more confident you will feel.

When you have a sense of assurance coursing through your mind, you believe in your ability to handle problems. This is a vital character trait to possess as it helps you to keep your cool and not panic when things don't go your way.

When Facing Change, Courage Is Your Best Friend

Once you have gained a certain degree of command over your courage and confidence, it is then time to build a certain strength as well.

It's a Bit Risky, Don't You Think?

Progress means that you have to start stepping out of your comfort zone, where it is probably warm and comfortable.

Think of your comfort as a nice log cabin. There's a warm fire crackling in the fireplace. The TV is on (this is a modern cabin, so don't worry about the details). You have a great internet connection and are able to access your favorite websites. A delicious meal awaits you, paired with a hot mug of tea or cider with steam that wafts through the air in swirls. Once you are done, you can crash on the comfortable bed that feels like it is made out of clouds.

Then you have the act of stepping out of your comfort zone. That's like leaving the warm, cozy, and beautiful cabin to embrace a biting cold and windy night. You have to venture out into the dark woods and there is barely any light. You also forgot your winter coat. You hear a howl in the distance and what might either be the cracking of a branch or the snapping of twigs as a malevolent entity approaches you (yes, your imagination might begin to run wild, so watch out for that). All in all, it's not a pleasant experience. You just want to be back in the safety of the log cabin.

But you still need to venture out into the harsh world, because that may hold an abundance of opportunity. You might find another log cabin, allowing you to discover new friends. You might come across a beautiful lake, giving you access to food, water, and a beautiful view.

DEALING WITH CHANGE IN YOUR PERSONAL LIFE

In life, you need to start taking steps to leave your comfort zone in order to either do great things or find something more.

You need to start taking risks.

But why take risks? Especially when there is the small chance that you might fail or face disappointments. So why do it in the first place?

The simple reason is that risk leads to a better life. You gain access to unforeseen opportunities. If you don't explore, you don't experience.

Your comfort zone is a wonderful place to rest. But that's all it offers – comfort (hence the name). Nothing grows there. You don't become better. Rather, you just remain in a stationary position.

When you take risks, you're able to become something. You can improve your condition. You can get the things that you want.

Then, there are the other reasons why you should be taking risks.

You begin to face your fears and failures. Your fear and the idea that you might fail keep you from doing something remarkable with your life. You become rooted to the spot, unable to even think of advancing in your life. However, life always brings you to a T-junction. You have to make a choice between staying safe by remaining where you are, or doing something to become something better, achieve something, or get what you want. At that point, it's your strength to take risks that will help you make the right choice.

It makes you successful. Speak to any successful person and tell them that their success might have come to them when they were in their comfort zone. They are more than likely going to laugh at you. Successful people know that if they are still doing the same things over and over again, they are not going to be better than they are. When Steve Jobs began to guide Apple, he decided to cut 70% of their product line, a risky move that could have shocked anyone else (Fell 2011). Why did he do it? Because he had a vision of success for himself and the only way to reach his goals was to make a risky move. In the end, it paid off. How else do you think Apple became the first trillion-dollar company in the world (BBC, "Apple First US Company to Be Valued at $2tn")?

It develops your self-confidence. Trying to have a constant supply of confidence can be fairly draining. For that reason, the more you begin to take risks, the more you become acclimated to facing bigger challenges. This, in turn, makes you aware that you are quite capable. Your self-confidence takes a huge boost, like it was strapped to a rocket sent into space. That boost further allows you to strengthen yourself against fears. After all, if you can take on such a big challenge, you're ready to take on more. It's a chain reaction of events that simply starts with one decision; to take a risk.

You learn. One of the biggest reasons to take risks is that it gives you valuable experience and knowledge. They help you understand what you should be doing and how to find alternative plans. Made a mistake? That's okay. Now you know what *not* to do. Learned something new? Use it to improve yourself.

You are rewarded. Do you truly seek that reward you have always been meaning to reach? It could be a prized job position, a fancy new car, a relationship with someone spectacular, spiritual enlightenment, or anything else you dream of getting. The harsh truth is that you will only get there if you are willing to take the risk necessary to jump-start that thing. Remember, get out of that log cabin.

With that being said, remember that there is such a thing as 'too much'. By taking risks, you are definitely improving your chances of success. However, there is also a curse that you need to be aware of: overconfidence.

Make sure that you understand your limits. For example, let's say that you have been practicing playing guitar, and you want to take the risk of performing live. Rather than jump into a local theatre or club to perform in front of hundreds of people, try holding a small concert by inviting your friends and family. This will allow you to understand what it feels like to play in front of a crowd. It will build your confidence, give you the opportunity to practice your music, and perhaps even allow you to brainstorm new ideas.

Take your time to analyze your risks so that you can gauge if your level of experience matches it, or if your output will be received favorably.

Then there is the problem of analysis paralysis. As we saw in Chapter 2 under the section of Failure, we might often over-analyze something until it prevents us from progressing. In such cases, you have one effective weapon.

A leap of faith.

When I used to host classes on self-improvement and on finding courage, I used to have many people ask me about the leap of faith.

They think it means that you have to "go big or go home." In their minds, they have this idea that they simply have to put all their time, effort, or other investments into a risky venture and go along with it no matter the consequences.

However, to me the concept of a leap of faith has a different meaning. For that reason, I have created a special exercise to help people find their courage to make the leap of faith happen.

Exercise #8: Faith Can Move Mountains

I once had someone who had participated in my classes tell me about the time that they had a strong desire to go snowboarding. But they were worried that they might end up in a horrible accident.

To them, I suggested a two-step process called the "Faith Pincer." The name utilizes the famous pincer movement – a military strategy where forces attack from two different directions at the same time – and applies that concept to faith.

So how does it work?

Step 1 (or Pincer 1): Confidence

In this step, you're going to learn how to build your skills or experiences. In the case of the would-be snowboarder, I asked them to first let me know if they had practiced snowboarding. This is an important step and as we learned earlier; you build confidence by putting into practice your skills and knowledge.

The would-be snowboarder said that they had indeed been practicing. If they had told me that they hadn't practiced much, then I would have told them to first try to improve their skill.

You build your defenses by building your confidence. It allows you to be sure of yourself and resist doubts or fear.

Step 2 (or Pincer 2): Attack

For this step to work, you need to know something I like to call the "faith jolt." Essentially, it's the point when you become hesitant about going forward or even turn around and avoid taking any action at all. It is that moment when fear, doubts, or even insecurities cloud your judgment and attempt to nullify your courage.

Make a note of that situation or feeling. Then create a move called "faith CPR." Essentially, you create a set of statements or affirmations that help remind you of what you're capable of. The affirmation should talk about your experience and help motivate you. The would-be snowboarder created this affirmation:

I have trained myself to be a snowboarder. I believe in my training. I have the confidence I need. I welcome the opportunity to stretch myself and have fun.

A fairly simple affirmation, isn't it? Yet the most important aspects of it are that it contains a fact about the person's skills or knowledge. By going with others and having their support, the would-be snowboarder even had a little solution tucked in his back pocket should things not work out well.

When the moment arrives where you find yourself frozen in indecision, then you simply have to say the affirmation out loud to yourself.

Remember that a leap of faith does not necessarily refer to big changes. It refers to each step you take or the little milestones you cross as you progress towards your goals.

But while you're building your courage and confidence, there is something else you should keep in mind as well.

Your humility.

6

Humility in Your Heart

Most people believe that change is an external force. However, while change does have external influence, most of it originates from deep within us. It's our skills, knowledge, experiences, and even memories that shape us. But along with them comes another factor that influences change: our flaws.

We carry our flaws with us nearly our entire lives. We are able to deal with some of them, while others remain persistent. All of these flaws tend to create the wrong idea about ourselves in our minds. They speak of the things we cannot do, the person we cannot be, or the fact that we are destined to fail despite our best efforts. They are a reminder of the worst situations.

Our flaws seem to get worse when we compare them to someone else which, let's face it, we do quite a lot. It's not easy to watch someone else get ahead in certain fields and increase the gap between you and them. It can make you feel inferior.

However, it's important to realize that others have progressed because they understand their strengths and weaknesses.

You might have heard of billionaires wearing simple outfits everyday. Some even look as though they are wearing the same clothes from one day to the next. There is a reason for them doing so. These billionaires have figured something out about themselves; they can't rely on their minds entirely. They know that their minds might create unnecessary stress when spending a considerable amount of time choosing their outfits. In order to avoid that stress early in the morning, they plan out their wardrobe for the next day or even the whole week in advance.

In other words, they have accepted their flaws and instead of rejecting them, the billionaires know it is better to work *with* them.

It's important to keep in mind that each person's journey is different. You cannot compare your goals to someone else because you both have different priorities, interests, backgrounds and abilities, and you might not face the same challenges. Neither would you share the same circumstances or network of people surrounding you and supporting you.

On the flipside is the idea of overconfidence. Some people think that they can just ignore their flaws and that they are beyond making mistakes. They overestimate their capability to perform. It's a bias that ignores one simple fact; they can get better, but they choose not to.

So, what can you do in such cases? How can you approach your flaws without fear or overconfidence?

You just need to employ humility. The importance of humility has been acknowledged by psychologists (Leary 2020), who note that it allows people to have an accurate view of themselves, especially their strengths and weaknesses. Humility teaches us various lessons, each of which is important for our growth.

Here are some of its vital lessons:

You are not perfect. But that's okay. You don't need to achieve perfection, just improvement. In fact, the issue with perfection is that it's merely an idea that does not have a concrete example. You could find something perfect, but it might not be the same for everyone else. Furthermore, perfection always seems like a distant point, after which one is often still dissatisfied and longs for more. It may be a cliché, but it's true that perfectionists are never content. Try to keep achievable targets. That way, you can place bigger targets after achieving the previous one.

You don't know everything. Always consider yourself a student, and not a master. That way, you are constantly looking to improve yourself. Telling yourself that you know everything means that there is nothing else for you to learn. That could be your downfall, since your existing skills and knowledge might not be able to match future demands and innovations.

Your feelings don't serve you. Remember what we learned about the subconscious mind – it's the emotional part of you that does not know better. You cannot rely on it to plan things out for yourself or to make your decisions. Make sure that you're using your rational mind to evaluate a situation, action, decision, or idea.

Accept your weaknesses. Don't allow your flaws to make your decisions. No matter what you do, try to evaluate the situation from a rational standpoint. Take into consideration all the pros and cons. Get more information, if possible. Don't allow your weaknesses to influence you.

There's nothing wrong with seeking outside help, such as from friends, family members, or even a professional therapist. The more you try to deny help, the more you are only going to prolong the situation you're in. Get help and get back on your feet.

You don't need to prove yourself all the time. There is not a lot of time for that. If people fail to see your value, then you should move on as you focus on your goal. You need to be secure in your own identity. You might notice that successful people don't really need to prove themselves to anyone. They continue making progress. To them, growth and change are their destination. They couldn't care less about what others have to say about them.

Not a Weakness

While we are talking about humility, let's address a fairly common misconception about the term.

People assume that humility indicates weakness or downplaying oneself. Somehow, you become an inferior version of you when you become humble. But the reality is far from such assumptions.

Humility does not equate to meekness or submission. It doesn't ask you to consider yourself lower than someone else. Neither does it signify that you are being self-effacing.

In fact, humility is considered a character strength. This is because it features three vital components: being empathetic, displaying modesty, and respecting others. However, before we go any further, I would like to delve into the idea of emotional intelligence.

For a long time, people often assumed that it took mere mental strength or knowledge to make a leader. Leaders had to outwardly display power and carry on with an almost cold, calculating, or ruthless persona. They had to act as emotionless statues, lest someone perceive them as weak or having cloudy judgment if their feelings got in the way. Science, on the other hand, is of a different opinion. Research has shown how emotional intelligence actually improves leadership effectiveness, not weakens it (Kerr et al. 2006). In fact, more studies have surfaced that prove that emotional intelligence is as crucial as our skills, knowledge, and experiences.

Just to be clear, emotional intelligence does not mean that you have to start wearing your heart on your sleeve and become an extremely emotional person. No, I'm not asking you to cry openly in front of everyone.

Emotional intelligence is the ability of an individual to perceive their emotions and be able to evaluate and control them. It's important to understand your own emotions so you are fully aware of your reactions. This allows you to use your emotions effectively, such as trying to stay calm when you feel as though you would like to get angry or avoiding feeling sad when it's not necessary. At the same time, emotional intelligence is also about interpreting and responding to the emotions of others.

One of the key components of emotional intelligence is empathy, which allows us to place ourselves into the shoes of others so that we can view the world through their eyes and understand what they are going through.

Emotional intelligence allows you to:

- Take criticism in a responsible manner by evaluating what the other person said rather than become defensive.
- Understand that you have made a mistake and that you should move on.
- Display modesty when required.
- Empathize with others and attempt to understand what they are going through.
- Share your feelings, no matter how difficult they might be, to others when required.
- Employ spectacular listening skills.
- Respect others and their opinions without bias.
- Recognize why you do the things that you do.

As you can see, emotional intelligence is critical for both understanding complex situations or people, knowing when to use tact or restraint, and coming into more self-awareness. Now I would like you to look back to see what we had understood when we were looking at the concept of humility. When we are humble, we:

- Are able to display modesty.
- Can empathize with others.
- Respect others.

Humility is a sign of strong emotional intelligence. All three of the above characteristics help us understand something truly important: that kindness and consideration for others have more of an impact than we realize, and people are more receptive to that than to a harsh brazenness. As the saying goes, "you'll catch more flies with honey than with vinegar." People can then also see our humility as a willingness to be more straightforward about our shortcomings, making us that much more trustworthy, reliable, and honest in their eyes.

Now comes the important part; just *how* can we develop humility?

Exercise #9: Humblebee

Humility teaches us that we don't have control over each and every situation. We can only do our best with the cards we have been dealt. Sometimes, that suffices. If you are going to stay up all night pondering about why you're not all that great and why things are not going your way because of your sheer awesomeness, then you are setting yourself up for failure.

There are three vital methods to develop humility. The first one is to simply improve your listening skills.

1. Listen Before You Speak

Start a conversation with someone. Pick a topic that you both are comfortable with and can contribute. This part is important because it serves as a challenge. Once the conversation is well underway, hold yourself back from saying anything. No matter how knowledgeable, funny, articulate, confident, or interesting you think your response is, don't say it. Instead, all you are going to do is encourage the other person to speak. Even if they are telling you something you already know, don't interrupt them. At the same time, pay attention to what they are saying. Ask them questions about what they said. Allow them to elaborate on points.

The more you repeat this exercise, even when you are having a conversation in a crowd, the more you will train yourself to listen with intent.

2. *Self-Compassion*

Identify your faults. Write them down in a journal or a note-taking app on your mobile device. Then try to be kind to yourself about these flaws. Let yourself know that having them does not make you inferior. Rather, they are opportunities that you can explore.

Think of your goals. Then think about which flaws you need to deal with in order to achieve your goals. Create an action plan to deal with them. As for the rest of the flaws, they don't matter. After all, they're not going to help you in any way. Dealing with them is not going to help you reach your goals, so why bother? Accept that they are part of the human experience and move on.

3. *Practice Mindfulness*

A simple way to master this method is by doing breathing exercises. When one thinks of breathing exercises or meditation, they often imagine carving out a 20-minute session. But that's not necessary. You simply have to give yourself a five-minute break to practice meditation.

One simple form of meditation is to find a comfortable position (whether sitting, standing, or lying down). You can keep your eyes open or closed. Simply inhale as you count to a certain number (let's say 6 for the sake of this example). Hold your breath for a few seconds and then exhale. Make sure that when you exhale, you are counting as well. The count for exhalations should be longer than the one you make for inhalations.

4. *Accountability*

Talking about accountability requires an in-depth knowledge and understanding about it, which is why we'll head to the next chapter to fully grasp its importance.

7

The Responsible Way - Be Accountable

Let's face it, we're not perfect. But nor are we meant to be.

We make mistakes. We stumble along the path of life and barely manage to keep ourselves upright as we navigate its twists, turns, and diversions. We become lost, then find the right way, and then become lost again. Such is the grand experience of life.

But let me tell you something important; all of that is okay.

You are meant to make mistakes. They teach you to become better. They show you what you shouldn't be doing.

You might discover that your actions often backfire, and they don't create the result that you had expected of them. Before we continue, I would like you to perform a simple exercise.

This exercise is going to help you understand your reactions, and we will be using it in a future exercise later in the chapter.

Exercise #10: Down Memory Lane

I'd like you to take yourself back to a time when you made a wrong decision. It doesn't have to be a major incident in your life, it can just be something you wish you had done differently. Your decision might have affected just you alone, or it could have had an impact on the lives of others as well. It doesn't matter if the decision you took was for a project in your university, a team task at work, or when someone depended on you to complete something. Whatever the stimulus, the end result was not something you were happy with.

Now consider what you did after you realized that your decision wasn't satisfactory.

Did you:

- Admit to your mistake and then take responsibility for your actions?
- Deflect blame or perhaps even avoid it entirely?

I'd like you to keep your answer in your mind. It will play a vital role in the next exercise. For now, I would like to delve into the importance of taking responsibility.

It Starts with You

When we were kids, we had a strong compulsion to avoid taking the blame. We understood the consequences of certain actions or decisions. We were either afraid of the punishment that would be doled out to us by adults, or we just didn't like the feeling of how wrong our actions made us feel. Naturally, in order to avoid discipline or the uncomfortable feeling of guilt, we would often refuse to take responsibility or stay in denial.

The Responsible Way - Be Accountable

We would flat out lie to people, even though our lies were rather obvious.

However, as we grow into adults, we usually shed some of the habits we had as children. Our perspective of the world shifts.

At this point, we would all like to believe that we are like the moth that turns into a butterfly; our adult life ushers in a new version of us, one that is more sensible or rational. Unfortunately, that's not how things work in reality. Many people carry their childhood habits well into adulthood.

Before we go any further, I would like to remind you that there are many reasons this might be the case, and it's not my place to judge anyone. Rather, I am merely showing the truth that situations may cause some of our past behaviors to seep into the present.

This also doesn't mean that you cannot change and that your past behaviors are like scars that are never going to leave you. That's untrue, and such ideas tend to keep you rooted to the spot. When you get rooted to the spot, then you begin to avoid change and stop taking risks.

So let's agree right now that we are not going to become enslaved to our past ideas and remain stagnant.

But what happens when we stop taking responsibility?

To put it simply, it might give you an advantage for a short time. For example, by not revealing something, you could get away with avoiding the consequences or punishment. However, things will eventually catch up to you, causing you to make a more difficult choice in the future.

There are also other consequences to avoiding responsibility. You might lose good friends or family, become acclimated to avoiding decisions, causing you to miss out on opportunities, make poor lifestyle and health choices, destroy your professional or personal life, or even end the possibility of achieving the goal you have been meaning to follow for a long time.

Your mistakes do come with a cost to you. But not taking responsibility to correct them or work towards improving yourself is going to make things worse.

Having understood what happens when we avoid taking responsibility, is there any advantage in taking it?

Yes, there is:

- Firstly, you push yourself out of the victim mode. You stop feeling sorry for yourself and start becoming a proactive person.
- You learn to gain more confidence in your abilities. You realize that, in the end, the only person who can control your actions and decisions is you. There's no one who's going to take your place. You can let that thought empower you to start taking charge of your decisions.
- You also learn to develop relationships. When you take responsibility, people will realize that you are a trustworthy person. If you make a mistake, you are more likely to receive help because others know that you are not going to just give up and shift blame.
- You might also become a role model for someone else. People may start looking up to you because they see a person of action, not a person living with inaction.

So, what are the steps that you can take to become a more responsible person?

Let's begin with the exercise.

Exercise #11: Who's Responsible for This?

Did you carry out the previous exercise? If you did, then think about your answer, because each of them will lead to a slightly different approach to this exercise.

If you chose the first option, which is to admit to your mistake and then take responsibility for your actions, then you can skip step 1 and head straight to step 2.

On the other hand, if you chose the second option, then worry not – that's completely okay. I was also the person who avoided responsibility for the longest time. It took a lot of understanding and practice to eventually break out of that mindset. Once I did, I began to become more confident in taking action.

1. Back to the Present

One of the reasons why people try to avoid responsibility is because their minds have already drifted into the future. They are considering the consequences of their decisions and all the disastrous events that are going to follow. But that only makes them think about the future, which is a place where anything is possible. I like to call this process "problem procrastination." You start thinking about what is going to happen in the future, not about what is currently happening in the present. Then your ruminations prevent you from actively doing anything about your current problem.

Instead, you should switch gears. Forget about the future, even if you are absolutely certain of the outcome. It hasn't happened yet, and so it doesn't matter.

Then you can start taking actions to try and resolve the issue.

I would also like for you to temper your expectations. Most people think of trying to completely resolve the issue. But what you don't know about mistakes is that they usually cannot be undone entirely. They are going to leave behind the marks of their effects.

You should train your mind to accept that you are aiming to minimize damage and contain the issue. Of course, you will eventually find a solution to tackle the problem. But the problem itself isn't going to completely remove all the consequences it created. For example, if you had sent the wrong email to a client, there is nothing you can do about the fact that said client has read the email. At this point, you shouldn't think of undoing anything; that will only lead to massive disappointments. Rather, you should focus on what you should be doing next.

So, what should you be doing next?

2. *Create SMART Goals*

Be SMART. I'm not referring to your psychological state because, let's face it, you *are* smart, you awesome person!

I am actually referring to a proven technique used to solve problems.

SMART is an acronym that stands for Specific, Measurable, Achievable, Relevant, and Time-bound.

Here's how it works in the context of solving a problem. Let's say that you were supposed to complete a project by a certain date and that you are slightly late.

The first thing that you should do is remember step 1; you cannot undo it. What has happened has happened and that's how things are going to be. At the same time, don't fall prey to the influence of problem procrastination. You don't have time to worry about what has yet to happen because what should occur in the future should remain in the future. No need to dredge it up and drag it into the present.

Thus, it is time to start creating SMART goals.

Specific: You should have a clear solution in mind. Don't just say something along the lines of "I want to stop being late on my projects." Rather, you should be saying, "I need to get back to my work. I need to figure out what I can do to complete my project. I also need to gauge how long it might take me to finish the project. Once done, I need to schedule out some time to focus. Most importantly, I need to start doing it immediately."

Measurable: Don't create arbitrary units of measurement to check the status of your goal. For example, don't say, "I'll aim to complete my project as soon as possible." What exactly does 'as soon as possible' mean? A day? Two days? One week? A month? A godly millennium?

Measure it. Your goal could be:

Take two hours every day to focus on the project. This will ensure that the project will be complete in 6 days. As a buffer—in case I have to deal with an emergency or I'm unable to meet my two-hour daily target—I will keep 8 days as the time it will take to complete the project in its entirety.

Achievable: This step is important. Once you have created your measurable goals, try to check if they are achievable as well. If you're reasonably confident you can work two hours a day, then go ahead and follow the course you've set for yourself. However, if you think that two hours is pushing it, then you might have to re-evaluate your plan.

On the other hand, when you think of the idea of achievability, you should also check to see if you are not making things too easy for yourself. Can you work three hours instead of two? Then why aren't you doing that? If there is a valid reason for only working for two hours, then you should stick to the schedule. But if there isn't, what's stopping you from doing a little more within your means?

Relevant: The relevancy of your goals also matters, since it helps you decide how much effort you truly need to put into a project.

One of the questions you can ask yourself is:

I have made a mistake. I am going to take full responsibility for that. But do I have to solve the issue right now? If this is a personal project, then why did I delay it for so long? Am I burning out? Is my creativity draining out? In that case, should I take a break instead?

Relevance also takes into consideration the concept of responsibility. For example, is this project only relevant to you? Is there anyone else involved in its completion? If there is, then shouldn't the other party (or parties) also contribute towards the completion of the project?

Time-bound: Finally, we look at the concept of time. As we have seen in the section about measurement, you calculated that you will be able to complete the project in 6 days. But make sure you are absolutely certain about that.

You could even modify your time-bound goal in this way:

I will aim to complete the project in 6 days. However, I believe that if I can manage to put in 3 hours every day, then I might be able to complete the

project faster. Additionally, I will also add a buffer period in case of any delays or issues that might occur. Based on my estimations, here are my time estimates:

- *Fastest delivery period: 4 days*
- *Expected delivery period: 6 days*
- *Adjusted delivery period: 8 days*

8

Navigating Through Negativity

Did you know that you can actually become addicted to negativity? In fact, I would like you to think about the thoughts you have during a typical day. How many positive thoughts do you have compared to the negative ones?

I'll harbor a guess that you might provide one of these answers:

- You have more negative thoughts than positive ones.
- You think that you are generally more positive.

If you had the first thought or response, then I am here to tell you that you share the same habit with billions of other people around your world, including your friends, family, and even your neighbors.

On the other hand, if you chose the second option, then let me respectively suggest that you might not be entirely honest with yourself.

According to one article posted in *Psychology Today* (Colier 2019), more than 80% of your thoughts are negative and up to 95% can be repetitive thoughts. I'll bet you didn't imagine the figures to be that high, right? Neither did I when I first stumbled across that fact. But over time, I tried paying attention to my own thoughts and, true enough, I had a lot of negative mental speech.

We are a generation that consumes a lot of media. We are bombarded with news and information so easily that all it takes is a few clicks to go from looking at the weather to watching a guitar tutorial to catching up on the news. However, you might notice that most of the information we consume is negative.

The news mainly focuses on the tragedies, disasters, crimes, and other dangers that occur around the world. Your favorite movies, tv series, and video games focus on violence, death, and misfortune. We face more challenges during the day than rewards.

In short, we are bombarded with so many negative situations, ideas, and stimuli that our mind becomes used to them. Additionally, we are also attached to negativity, in a way. We resonate more with the struggles in our lives and the obstacles we have to overcome, and then we relate tales of how we overcame adversity because they help define us in a better light.

However, if we are not able to counterbalance the negativity within us, then we might just become accustomed to it. All of the thoughts that serve to bring us down might end up becoming constant companions, perhaps even friends, as we begin to rely on them heavily.

Eventually, you start to create negative self-talk. This eventually spirals into a rather tricky situation where you begin to rely on prolonged negativity.

According to researchers from the Institute of Psychiatry, Psychology & Neuroscience (IoPPN) at King's College London (King's College London 2014), prolonged exposure to negative thoughts actually impairs and restricts our brain's ability to form memories, reason, and even think normally. This means that we might start looking at things through a filter that actually limits the flow of positive stimuli.

Moreover, negative self-talk can lead to a host of unfavorable issues that include:

- Labelling ourselves, usually in a poor light.
- Creating all-or-nothing ultimatums. In this situation, we consider ourselves failures, weak, or disappointing, or we stick other negative ideas on ourselves simply because we couldn't reach a certain goal. We don't care to look instead at the progress we've made.
- We have a mental filter that prevents us from appreciating the good things in life.
- We easily jump to conclusions without taking the big picture into consideration.
- We indulge in the process of catastrophizing, where we blow a single incident out of proportion and make it seem more terrible than it actually is.
- We take things personally. Even reasonable criticism might sound like someone is insulting us rather than helping us improve.

But there's more. Yes indeed. Negative self-talk can affect us in a lot of other ways.

You might end up with **limited thinking processes**. This does not mean that you're not knowledgeable or that you're incapable of improving yourself. What it means is that, despite the knowledge you have, you only have a fixed view on things, restricting your ability to absorb valuable information and ideas. One of the results of this limited view is our mental bias friend, confirmation bias.

Because we have such a narrow view on things, we also start believing in the idea of **perfectionism**. After all, we give ourselves all-or-nothing ultimatums. This means that we have a certain idea of what we should achieve; and if that doesn't happen, we become disillusioned and disappointed. We stop looking at the number of steps we have taken forward and become fixated on the number of steps that still remain.

Eventually, all of the negative ideas and self-talk affects our mental health. We become **depressed**. This eventually turns into a vicious cycle: our depression makes us look at life from a negative viewpoint, which continues to feed our self-talk, which eventually causes even more depression. It's like a mental ouroboros, your mind feeding itself on negativity and spewing that same negativity out.

What do you think happens when we have such a tumultuous frame of mind? Well, we begin to take it out on others, becoming distant or cold towards them. We might ignore our friends or become downright rude to our family members. Even though our loved ones may reach out to us, we're like a ticking time bomb; no one knows when we might display a burst of negative emotion. Our negativity eventually attacks our **relationships**.

So how do we stop this cycle of self-hate, self-blame, and other self-inflicted mental injuries? What can we do to evolve into a person who is capable of evaluating things rationally and looking at the bright side of things (at least more often)?

Exercise #12: Two Negatives Don't Always Make a Positive

1. From the Unconscious to the Conscious

Do you want to know the main reason why many people are unable to deal with their negative self-talk?

It's simple; this kind of negativity mainly occurs in your subconscious. Have you ever wondered how some of your thoughts appear in your head? Do you know the entire process? Are you aware when your brain takes an idea, converts it into thought and projects it into your mind?

No, you're probably completely unaware of this process because it all happens in your subconscious; and your thought just appears in your head, doesn't it?

It's the same with negative self-talk. It just pops into your head and you're left dealing with the aftermath. We can't exactly catch it before it appears. That's because the subconscious mind's influence is the strongest when you are least aware of it. That's why we shouldn't be aiming to catch our self-talk, but rather to find defenses against it.

To do so, we need to record our negative self-talk. Whenever you have one or more of those pessimistic, self-defeating thoughts, try to write them down immediately or make a mental note of what the thought said to you so that you can record it later. Don't do anything with these thoughts. Just write them down without judgment or complaint. Continue doing this for a whole week so that you exhaust all the negative thoughts your subconscious mind is able to push into your consciousness.

2. Translate the Thoughts

Once you have recorded all the negative self-talk, imagine your best friend, loved one, or family member. Ask yourself; if you were their subconscious, would you tell them all the things that your own subconscious has told you?

For example, let's say that your subconscious has been telling you that you are a complete idiot. Would you say the same thing to your friend or someone close to you?

When you mirror the words of your subconscious into another situation that involves others, then you might start looking at your thoughts in a different way. This simple process will make you feel completely aware of your negative self-talk. The next time they appear, it might feel as though they were being said to your friend or loved one and not to you. That idea alone will make you rethink how you talk to yourself.

3. Reprogram Your Thoughts

There are two ways to do this.

Imagine that your friend came to you and said that someone had spoken to them the way that your subconscious mind speaks to you. For example, if your negative self-talk had told you that you are a failure, then imagine your friend telling you that someone had called them a failure. How do you respond? What advice do you give them? How do you convince them that they are not what they have been told?

Use the same advice on yourself. The more you remind yourself of the responses you have created, the more you are able to reprogram your negative self-talk with an improved response that is filled with motivation, hope, and perhaps even optimism.

The other method is to actually ask for help from your friends or family. Ask them what they would say if someone called you a failure (or whatever else it is that your mind tries to tell you). Get their perspective. Try to encourage them to give you advice on what you can do to move forward or show yourself more love.

People usually find it easy to offer advice to others, and, by that logic, your friends and family should be able to provide feedback for you.

A Sense of Fatigue and Hopelessness

Negativity does not only cause emotional turmoil, but it can lead to emotional fatigue as well.

Due to all the negativity it holds, your mind is frequently under the influence of stress. The more stress you accumulate, the more mental exhaustion you gather as well. Eventually, you reach a point where you feel overwhelmed, emotionally fatigued, and mentally drained.

This is a rather dangerous situation to be in. For one, your mental prowess is not particularly strong when you're in that state. You have no power to defend yourself against negativity, which attacks you in full force. This means that you allow it to cause wreckage in your mind, unimpeded.

It's almost like inviting a guest to your home and watching them destroy the furniture while you stand there exhausted because you haven't slept in days.

Feeling overwhelmed will, in turn, also affect the way you deal with stress. Typically, stress is a useful mechanism, since it activates your fight-or-flight mode when you feel threatened. However, the more you activate this response, the poorer your judgment becomes. It's a self-generating cycle; your negative thoughts cause you to experience stress, which makes you feel as though there is a threat in the environment. So you end up feeling anxiety for no reason.

Eventually, you become used to this level of emergency response to a point where you begin to ignore your fight-or-flight instincts.

At this point, let's o deal with two different mental states –stress and anxiety.

What do we do about them? Let's start with stress.

Excess Of Stress

Step 1

By simply saying that you have stress, you are essentially creating a broad situation that could mean practically anything. It doesn't allow you to tackle the problem effectively because, frankly, you might not know what it is you need to be dealing with in the first place. Stress can stem from a variety of causes.

Your first course of action is to discover all the situations, people, ideas, activities, plans or goals that are causing you stress. As with the previous exercise on negativity, try to keep a journal of some kind to record various stress triggers throughout the week. These triggers are going to help you identify where you should focus your attention and what you should be ignoring.

Step 2

While you're recording all the triggers, try to also note the ways in which you respond to such triggers. What do you do in order to deal with stress? Do you smoke cigarettes or drink? Do you binge watch TV series for long hours? Do you simply lie down in bed without doing anything?

When you're able to identify your responses, you're also able to manage them. If you haven't identified them and have no control over them, you might well give them the ability to control you when you're least aware of it.

Step 3

Replace unhealthy habits. Often, stress causes you to depend on your bad habits. This might include unhealthy eating, poor sleep patterns, venting your anger on someone else, procrastination, and other unhelpful actions. Eat healthy, practice a form of yoga or meditation, and try to exercise frequently. These are small habits that might seem like an obvious inclusion in your life, but you would be surprised how many people don't do them.

Step 4

When you have made the little changes in your life, you are creating the foundation for the big changes that are about to take place.

These appear in the form of replacements. What are some of the activities that cause stress? Remove them. If they're important to your goals, then think about how you can deal with them effectively or counterbalance their effects with things that you enjoy doing that relieve the pressure.

For example, if you've been working all day, and the work has been particularly stressful, then when you return home, avoid any thoughts about work. Instead, have a good meal, spend time with friends, or play a video game, if you're into that. Allow your stress to drop out of your system before you do anything else. Taking breaks, having time to rest (physically and mentally) and to do things you enjoy are just as essential as the myriad of serious responsibilities you have on your plate. Relaxation is a form of recharging so that your life is not all work and no play, and it allows you to remember to just have fun sometimes. Remind yourself again that you are worth more than your productivity, and that you're not a cog in a wheel. There's more to life than that.

Step 5 (Optional)

What happens if the stress shoots up to unmanageable levels suddenly and you're unprepared for it?

If you have been changing your habits, then you will already be able to deal with such stress in a logical manner. However, if you start feeling overwhelmed, then simply follow these steps:

- Stop. Breathe. Don't worry about the problem because it seems as though butting your head against it isn't going to accomplish anything.
- Ask yourself this question: do you have a solution to the problem? If you do, can you implement it? If you're unsure, take a minute or two to think about some possible solutions. Are there any? If you can think of a solution, focus your attention on it rather than the problem. You will notice that your stress will slowly begin to abate the more confidently you work on your problem.
- If you don't have a solution, then walk away from the problem. There's nothing you can do. Instead of wasting time on worrying about the problem and your lack of ability to solve it, focus on changing your mindset.
- Take a break. Earlier I showed you a simple breathing exercise. You can use that to distance yourself from the issue in order to gain some much-needed clarity.
- Then, you can either postpone the problem for another time or you can return to it, but with a more rational mindset.

Anxiety Variety

My struggle with anxiety was a long one. Since I was occupied with work, I always used to blame the work pressure for the growing sense of unease and dread I would suddenly feel. I would be in a taxi heading home when my fight-or-flight instincts would flare up. My anxiety would frequently cripple me and hold my life hostage.

It was only after almost a year of torturous days that I decided to actually tackle a problem, thanks to something my friend mentioned to me. He talked about how we are the ones who are in charge of our lives, including our mental health. While we may not be able to do anything about the thousands of stimuli that we face each day, we can definitely control the way we react to them. However, most of the time we don't take a moment to understand what is going on with us; we just accept things as they are.

His words hit me like a freight train.

It was then that I realized that perhaps my unease, discomfort, and panic attacks that I would often experience were a sign of something much more problematic.

After talking to a professional, I discovered that I had anxieties that were caused by a multitude of reasons. Of course, I hadn't discovered those reasons yet, but eventually I did by using a simple exercise.

Exercise #13: Why So Anxious?

I would like to begin by saying that if you have extreme anxiety that could be the result of a mental health issue, then you need to reach out to a professional. In fact, this idea of seeking help applies to all mental health conditions, including depression and mania. Don't ignore the symptoms and avoid doing anything about them. While there is certainly nothing bad and nothing wrong with you if you struggle with these matters, it can certainly debilitate you to the point where it does affect your life, and you will need some sort of intervention to get a hold on your weaknesses.

While the exercises and techniques in this book might help you gain some control over your issues, they cannot replace the guided help of a professional.

Having said that, let's move on to the exercise itself.

One of the many reasons why your anxieties persist is because you generally tend to avoid your fears instead of tackling them head-on. This causes your fears to grow into a monstrous presence in your mind – one that should always be avoided.

Rather than running away from your fear, try and face it.

An ideal way to face your fears is by analyzing it rationally. Here's how you do it.

You perform a SWOT analysis.

I know what you're thinking; aren't SWOT analyses meant for businesses to gauge their competition and then find a way to stay ahead in the market? Yes they are. But perhaps you don't realize how powerful a tool it can also be when you use it to analyze your fear. All you have to do is consider your fear as a competitor that is preventing you from staying ahead in your life. The only difference is that this competitor is not above using underhanded and dirty tactics to keep you down.

Let me show you how you can use SWOT analysis on your fears by using an example from my life. Remember that anxiety that was crippling my life? Here's how I discovered more about it.

SWOT is an acronym for Strengths, Weaknesses, Opportunities, and Threats. Here is how I applied this analysis technique to my anxiety problem.

Strengths

This section focuses on the strengths of the anxiety you are dealing with. In my case, I had the following list:

- It has been affecting me for a long time, so it has definitely grown in power.
- It attacks me suddenly, even when I'm taking a walk down the road.
- I can see that I haven't been paying attention to it, so I'm still not sure what I can do to deal with it.
- I feel like a lot of the anxiety is a result of my work, which is something I cannot avoid.

Weaknesses

This section highlights all the possible weaknesses of your anxiety. How do you discover a weakness? Well, you look at *your* strengths.

- I have finally become aware of it, which will allow me to deal with it.
- I don't have to fear it because I know that there is a solution for the problem.
- I have a good number of friends that I can rely on.
- I have talents that I can use to help me calm down.
- I also have access to breathing techniques that I can use to manage my anxiety.
- There are various therapists who can help me should I really require external help.

Opportunities

Here, we can take a look at all the opportunities that you can use to improve your life.

- I may not be a good cook, but I'm curious about trying out healthy food recipes. This should help avoid junk.
- I can remove junk food and stock my refrigerator with healthy fruits and vegetables. That way, if I feel the urge to eat my anxiety away, I will at least eat good food.
- I have a pleasant park near my home that allows me to take a nice brisk walk in the morning and enjoy nature.
- I have recently acquired a great book that will help me deal with my anxieties (hopefully in your case, it's this book).
- I'm going to start being more aware of my anxiety so that it does not seem like an unknown presence in my life.
- If I need it, I can have the help of my friends.
- I can easily access information on yoga, meditation, and other techniques, should the need arise.

Threats

In this section, we will look at all the ways your anxiety can pose a threat to you by deeply understanding it. I recommend taking a week to record when your anxieties strike you. I've provided a list of questions you can use after this exercise. Once you have a general idea of how your anxiety behaves, you can use this section.

- My anxiety is most frequent at work.
- I realize that thoughts about work also create anxiety within me.
- When I'm heading home from work, I dread any messages I receive from my colleagues or bosses.
- I know that I haven't found a proper solution to dealing with my anxiety, so I worry that I may not be able to deal with it if it decides to attack me spontaneously.

Here's the questionnaire that I use to better understand my anxiety. You could call it a journaling method; I use the questions to record my experiences for an entire week every time I experience anxiety.

- When did the anxiety occur?
- What was I doing at that moment?
- Was there a trigger that I can recall? For example, a phone call, bumping into a stranger who got upset, not being able to have my morning coffee that I so depend on?

NOTE: Coffee itself can be a trigger for anxiety because of the caffeine it contains. Also, you don't have to list just one trigger; you can add as many as you have for this question.

- Can I recall what I was thinking about at that moment?
- Was there something I was supposed to do or was in a hurry to complete?
- Was I already stressed about something at that moment? For example, a deadline, an upcoming meeting, etc?

Once you're able to discover more information about your anxiety, you can plug your responses into the Threat section of the SWOT analysis. Remember, your triggers can stem from more serious, deeper issues *or* they can be from perfectly trivial things.

Once you have developed some understanding about your anxiety, you can then focus on dealing with it. In my case, when I discovered that my anxieties were mainly because of my work, here are some of the solutions I came up with:

- I could change jobs. I feel as though I have been in this company long enough, and it's time for a change. Plus, my salary hasn't really increased all that much when compared to my experience.
- I would benefit from a lot more personal time as well. I need to find ways to shut off after I leave work rather than try to work even more when I reach home. I need to learn how to unwind.
- I haven't taken a holiday in quite a while. I think this is a sign that I definitely need a long break for myself.
- There might be something at work that's causing me all this anxiety. Can I find better ways to deal with those tasks or projects? Maybe I could approach them from a different angle and see how it works out.

That's An Imposter

The harmful influences of negative self-talk do not end only in stress and anxiety. They create another psychological situation called 'imposter syndrome.'

Imposter syndrome refers to a phenomenon where individuals begin to doubt their abilities and often think of themselves as a fraud. They don't feel like they genuinely have any skills to offer, and they worry they are unable to fulfil a responsibility entrusted to them. They feel like an imposter inhabiting the skin of another person who is supposed to be more equipped, capable, talented, intelligent, charismatic, honest, or any other characteristic we would like to have.

This psychological situation usually creates feelings of anxiety, discomfort, and self-doubt, especially at the workplace or when you are focused on an important task. You are unable to realistically evaluate your skills and knowledge, usually underestimating yourself. You strongly berate yourself for your performance rather than thinking of improving yourself, recognizing what you *can* do right, and realizing the actual skills and talents you *do* have. More importantly, you become the saboteur of your own success.

Eventually, you become your own worst enemy.

That thought is not an easy one to admit, and in order to counter this feeling, you become fixated on a 'solution.'

I remember a time when I had to meet some of my friends for dinner. I was so nervous about the whole endeavor that I began to feel anxiety. I began to doubt my ability to have a conversation. In order to prevent embarrassment that hadn't even occurred yet, I began to memorize a few cool facts that I could mention to my friends because I thought they would make me look interesting. Eventually, I became so fixated on telling those facts that I didn't pay attention to my friends or the conversation, and I certainly didn't enjoy myself or have a good time socializing with them.

All of this because I had no confidence in my abilities.

That's what happens to most people who are under the influence of imposter syndrome; they don't know how to escape their mental prison, so they invent solutions that don't solve the root of the problem, or in fact, solve anything at all.

So how can you tell if you have imposter syndrome? Is it merely about self-doubt? Not exactly. There are a few signs that you can look out for when trying to self-diagnose with imposter syndrome. Remember that you have to be very careful when you are self-diagnosing yourself with anything, since a wrong diagnosis might convince your mind of something that never existed before. I recommend seeking professional help if you feel like you need a second opinion or if your condition seems to be getting worse.

The first sign that you might notice is the abundance of **self-doubt**. You become fearful of taking charge of the changes in your life. Even though you're in a good position to work with the changes you face, you don't do it. You feel as though you are not capable of doing anything.

The second sign that you should look out for is the desire to be a **perfectionist**. Here's the problem with perfectionism; no one knows what that looks like. Everyone's idea of perfection varies. What you should be doing is conceptualizing in your mind a certain goal, and then work your way towards it. On your journey, you might be faced with challenging circumstances that will cause you to have to re-evaluate your habits, ideas, strategies or even to leave behind old methods. All of this becomes necessary if you genuinely want to succeed. After all, they are all changes you should welcome to be better.

However, when you are a perfectionist, you cannot stand such changes. You become obsessed with the idea that if things don't go a certain way, then that means they are flawed.

Another sign is a strong aversion to feeling as if you are being **judged**. Well, I suppose this is true for many people. However, if you have imposter syndrome, then you tend to think of all feedback as a form of judgment. Did someone tell you that there is a better way for you to solve a problem? That person is definitely judging you. Maybe you were offered constructive criticism. Nope, that's definitely judgment. Or how about advice from a more experienced person? Judgment day, my friends! Moreover, you also have this constant fear that you might be **discovered**. For what exactly? Even you might have no idea. Because of your extreme self-doubt, you create faults within yourself that don't exist and worry about those nonexistent flaws.

Finally, you **refuse to acknowledge your own success**. It isn't that you're humble or honest. It's just that you don't even want to take credit for your share of the work, and you play down your accomplishments. You might have discovered that aliens live deep within the supermassive black hole in the center of our galaxy, but when presented with the opportunity to accept a Nobel prize for your work, you respond with "It's not necessary. Not such a big deal, anyway." Being proud of your work is not a bad thing – it's important for your personal development. You may not want to boast about your accomplishments, and that's an understandable trait, but you

should still take the credit for the things you have done and for all your excellent, hard work. After all, you deserve it.

So how do we combat imposter syndrome?

Exercise #14: Finding the Imposter

Don't Set Unreachable Goals

Many people are of the opinion that if they don't have grand goals, then that means they are not setting themselves up for massive success. But that's a flawed way of thinking. This is because things change, and you cannot always pursue the same target. When you create unreachable goals, not only are you setting yourself up for disappointment early on, but you're preventing yourself from actually making measurable progress.

Understand Your Limits

Every person has a limit. That's okay. It's part of what makes us human. When you have a limit but you would like to do more and to exceed that limit, focus on improving your skills or knowledge accordingly. Instead of simply taking on more challenging tasks without understanding your capabilities, try to recognize the level of experience that is required to manage those tasks. Then improve yourself slowly before you commit to them or work on them.

Set a Time Goal

Don't just spend endless hours on a project. Make sure that you identify how long you should be working on a project in order to complete it and then use that as your duration. If the project is large, then divide it into manageable chunks. Give yourself time to relax after completing the project as well, and take short breaks in between. During your work period, pay complete attention to the project. When you're able to manage your time in an efficient manner, you won't allow it to go to waste, and as a result you'll feel a better sense of accomplishment.

Recognize What You Are Good At

There are two ways you can do this. The first is to remember that if you face an issue or problem, then it does not mean that you are automatically a failure. It simply means that you just found a way to improve your skills.

The second is to make sure you also give yourself time to focus on hobbies or passions that you are good at. It could be anything, from gardening to first-person shooter video games. A gentle reminder that you are indeed awesome is always welcome.

It's Perfect to Be Imperfect

Realize that no one is perfect. Even the people you admire all have their faults. Look deep enough and you might just discover them.

If you are idolizing someone in a way that makes them seem flawless, then your idea of them is flawed. You need to understand that people don't display their imperfections outright, obviously. Even though, for all intents and purposes, a person may appear absolutely spotless in character when in the presence of others, I guarantee they are an entirely different human being in private. Make sure you understand that and temper your expectations about someone, because while we all have strengths and good things about ourselves, we all have our struggles, too.

Similarly, allow yourself to accept the fact that you may not be perfect as well. Because, really, who wants that? If everyone in the world were perfect, then no one would need to look for better things to aim for. Humanity would never need to aim for the stars and discover unbelievable or new, exciting things. After all, we're perfect, aren't we?

Allow yourself to make mistakes and grow, and be okay with that. Don't beat yourself up too much.

But while we're on the topic of growth, it's time to understand exactly what that means.

9

As You Grow, You Experience Life

How does one grow?

Of course, I don't mean physically. But how do you grow as a person?

To me personally, and after years of battling my own flaws, I think it's the ability of a person to be open-minded about themselves. After all, you can only grow if you think that there is something that needs growth.

But before we delve deeper into the idea of growth, perhaps we should examine the concept from a bird's-eye point of view. More importantly, how is it different from change?

Change vs. Growth

There is a difference, it's just quite tricky to point it out because the more you think about it, the more the two words begin to blend into each other. This is specific to the idea of personal growth, where the two words could mean one and the same idea.

Let's look at change. Usually, the term refers to a shift, which could occur in a different way. You might want to change your college or city. You might want to change your personality. There are various ways in which you can go from one way of being to another. Your change can also be a one-time event. For example, when you lose a job, it definitely changes your life, but it's not a continuous process. You don't go back to your job and get fired again every single day. Furthermore, change does not have to be internally imposed every time. Sometimes, things happen that are beyond our control. Such events can shift our perspective or our lives in ways that we might be able to predict or might just surprise us.

Now let's focus our attention on growth. One of the major features of growth is that it's a gradual process. It does not usually occur overnight. It doesn't matter what kind of growth you're working on; from paradigm shifts that affect the way you think to events that shape you as a person, they all require incremental steps towards progress. And for good reason. Growth needs time to mature, since it usually brings with it a collection of lessons, insights, ideas, and suggestions that are valuable to you. Above all, growth is an internal process. It is a realization of or reflection on your thought processes and serves to compare where you are to where you were. It's a matter of learning. It's all in your hands; whether you are able to succeed or whether you are going to give up. Since growth is a gradual process, it also requires more courage, humility, and emotional intelligence than actual change requires.

I know that last statement might have prompted raised eyebrows in some of you. How can growth require more emotional control and maturity than change?

Here's why. While change does require a lot more of the essential, necessary traits we discussed, it requires them for a particular period so you can adapt and then move on. Once the change occurs, then you feel better. On the other hand, growth requires consistent emotional intelligence over a long period of time. This makes it a lot more challenging because you have to ensure you supply it with the required emotional raw materials even during the unpleasant moments in your life. It's more a shift in attitude than anything.

So, in light of everything we know, how do we enter the growth phase? More importantly, how do we break out of our personal comfort zones and then set forth into the adventurous realms of the territory of growth?

Exercise #15: Grow-Off

In order to accept personal growth, you need to start with your mindset. There are various ways to shift your perspective to avoid focusing on your comfort zones and actively engage with your growth zones.

Learn New Skills

There are many things you can learn, such as a different language, a new craft, or even develop some unique talent you may have. The more you engage with ideas and activities that are different or unfamiliar, the more you feel motivated to try new things in general. Your fear of experimenting and adventuring will begin to diminish.

A bonus idea you can focus on is to improve your existing skills. Try to use them in challenging ways. Discover new methods to improve what you already know.

For example, if you enjoy painting, then try a method you have never done before and use tools you haven't yet experimented with. This gives you a sense of confidence. You begin to trust yourself more, and it expands your repertoire of skills.

Create Challenges

You can do this with a friend, or you can do it alone. The process involves setting a specific further challenge for yourself when you discover that you're getting better at a particular skill.

For example, let's say that you can cook an awesome pasta dish that has impressed a lot of people. Maybe you can challenge yourself to recreate a Michelin-star pasta recipe using different ingredients. Give yourself a time limit as well.

Alternatively, you can even challenge someone else. For example, if you have been working out, you can challenge your friend or acquaintance to a certain goal, such as a race to successfully complete 50 pushups.

I am also a big fan of RAGs. What are they? RAG is short for Really Audacious Goal. Every so often, try to create a goal that is quite challenging and requires a fair amount of effort from you. For example, let's say that you are a writer whose word count averages at around 2,000 words per day. Push yourself to write at least 5,000 words one day.

These sudden bursts of challenge will really spur you on to achieve more. Even if you don't reach the ultimate goal you have set, you should have performed at least better than your average. The more you practice RAGs, the more you feel as though you are better than average. That feeling alone motivates you to look at yourself in a different light.

Be Aware of Your 'Blind Spots'

Medically, blind spots refer to the regions in your vision your eyes are not capable of seeing. Using that concept, a blind spot in your personality or character refers to a trait or feature that you are not aware of.

For example, I was never aware of the fact that I had what I like to call 'automatic pessimistic reaction.' No matter what happened or how good the news was, I would always look at it from a negative viewpoint. It was only when I became aware of it that I was able to change. What is your blind spot that you've been ignoring? It could be your anger, frustration, envy, or other traits that activate automatically without you fully realizing it.

Accept Your Flaws

Noticing your blind spots is just the first part of the process. You need to accept the flaws that you do notice and then make sure that you deal with them. Don't let them grow and develop into an even bigger problem in the future. It's okay if it takes time to deal with them or bring them down to manageable levels. What's more important is that you're paying attention to them.

Every time you notice their presence, try to rationally ask yourself if it's important for you to experience them at that moment. For example, let's say that you get easily irritated if you bump into someone on the street. The next time you fall into that situation, ask yourself if it is worth your effort and time to focus on such trivial emotions. After all, there are many other things you could – and perhaps should – be focused on that are far more crucial.

Stay Away From Negative People

Try to befriend or acquaint yourself with people who motivate and inspire you. Avoid people who are a constant source of negativity in your life or are energy vampires. If you have a close friend who is quite a negative person, then you can encourage them to improve themselves or just engage with them when you're doing something fun or positive.

Manage Your Ego

Make sure that you're not letting an inflated ego do the talking. It's okay to be proud of yourself, but that pride should not become so excessive that it's beyond your control or you feel as if you have no faults. An overinflated ego will convince you that you are superior to others.

When you start letting your ego control the show, you automatically begin to compare yourself to others. Two things can happen as a result of this comparison:

- You think that you are better than others. This causes you to believe that there is no need for you to improve. After all, if you admit to yourself that you're not the best, then you have to accept that you're not as fantastic as you had originally imagined. This leads to a state of stagnation. Even when you notice others

improving themselves and perhaps even exceeding your skills, you end up being in denial of the situation.
- You could even start to look at yourself in a poor light. You might notice that others are better than you and that your skills are poor or average, at best. This causes you to look at yourself negatively. You begin to think that it doesn't matter if you put in any effort since the results are going to be the same; you're not going to be that good.

While we are on the topic of ego, let's look at ways that we can deal with it.

10

Don't Let Your Ego Empower You

Do you want to know our biggest obstacle towards change?

Well, all you have to do is stand before a mirror and look straight at it!

Of course, it's you, yourself. Our egos are often filling our minds with biases, fallacies, and misinformation just to keep us on a certain track.

Your ego likes to adopt a state of least resistance whenever possible. It wants to avoid any challenges and prefers if you don't do anything at all. Consider just lying on the sofa all day and munching on fat-filled and sugar-filled foods. Your ego is going to give you two thumbs up of approval.

It will do everything in its power to prevent you from confronting your reality and questioning it. In fact, I would even say that your ego is like a totalitarian state, causing you to stop questioning anything so you don't realize the truth. Better a comfortable lie than a truth that requires hard work, right?

The more you pay attention to your ego, the more you fall into its trap. Just to be absolutely clear, your ego isn't by default an evil force to be reckoned with. You need it to conduct an overall evaluation of yourself and to build your self-confidence. It should be used to your benefit.

However, things take a turn for the worst when your ego starts dictating the terms because you can then fall into one or many of its traps.

There are 5 ego traps that you need to be aware of:

Trap 1: Avoiding negative feedback

No one is beyond receiving negative feedback. Even people you see in movies or videos whom you consider to be nearly perfect are not immune to negative feedback. Only those whose egos have become overinflated so that they completely dominate their minds consider themselves absolutely immune to any form of criticism.

Here's the reality of the situation: just because you receive negative feedback, it does not mean that you, as a person, are a failure. Rather, the feedback is on the work that you do, the skills you have, or the knowledge that you possess. You can use this information to improve yourself.

Remember that there are two kinds of feedback: constructive criticisms and personal attacks. If someone points out a fault in your skills and abilities, take your time to evaluate their point of view. Sure, it isn't easy to consider it, but there could be an opportunity to improve. On the other hand, if you receive a personal attack, then you can point out to the person that they have said something to offend you.

Trap 2: Becoming too comfortable with flattery

It is absolutely okay to accept compliments. After all, if you have done something to deserve praise, then why not accept it? However, you shouldn't depend on flattery to make decisions or form reactions. More importantly, flattery shouldn't be responsible for feeding your ego.

Here's an example. Let's say that you have completed a project. Someone comes to you and congratulates you on a job well done. That's absolutely okay. But it's not okay when you don't receive any feedback, and you begin to look down on yourself as a result, become frustrated, or have insidious negative thoughts about other people. When that happens, it's your ego that has taken over. Now I'm not saying that you shouldn't be looking for recognition; you deserve it, after all. But you shouldn't allow whether or not you get praise to change your viewpoint, your goals, or your future plans.

Trap 3: Addicted to control

There are some things that we have control over and others that we can't do anything about. This is the reason why most of our efforts should be diverted to the things that we can change.

But there is a crucial point to remember here; things may not always go our way.

It doesn't matter how much we try, our plans, goals, ideas, and actions are going to be influenced by outside forces. A simple example would be a desire to go to the gym every day. But what happens when something like a nationwide emergency causes all gyms to be shut down? Now imagine that you decide that – because you need to have absolute control – you're not going to exercise unless a gym is open. You might begin to make demands to the landlord to open the gym or you are going to cause a ruckus.

In the above situation, you are forcing control when it isn't possible. Instead, you should seek to discover alternate solutions. Workout at home, for example. See if you can invest in some exercise equipment. Find objects apart from gym equipment that you can use to work out. Look at videos online that show many people who have built a healthy lifestyle using items they find at home and without access to expensive gym equipment, special food, or supplements.

Trap 4: Refusal to acknowledge change

This point, in some ways, ties to the previous point.

When faced with change, don't try to avoid it. To avoid this trap, you should be seeking to let go of control when it's not required.

You need to become fluid, like water. Allow yourself to look at different avenues for success so that you open yourself to the chance of finding a better way to accomplish your goals. You might even learn a new skill or find another opportunity.

Trap 5: Forming false promises

Don't make a promise you can't keep.

This usually happens when you cannot realistically assess yourself or your goals, and you allow your ego to take charge. Let's say that you have just begun your writing journey. You have no idea how many words you can write per day, and that doesn't include the research you need to conduct for your writing. It's a moment of discovery.

Rather than humbly accept that you will gauge your skills, experience, and knowledge after writing for at least a week, you instead choose to believe that you are simply awesome. How? Well, your inflated ego told you so. You don't need an evaluation or a learning period. Those things don't apply to your sheer magnificence. In such scenarios, you start making promises to yourself. You think that you can easily write 5,000 words per day. But that isn't you talking, that's your overblown ego doing the talking for you.

Prevent your ego from making too much noise—whether that noise is puffing you up excessively or even pushing you down. Instead, keep a level head as you approach various problems and always allow rationality to prevail in the end.

So, how can we keep our egos in check?

Exercise #16: Me, Myself, and I

To begin with, you need to first remove all the mental food that ego likes to feed on. Let's look at how this can be done.

Procrastination

When you procrastinate, you allow your subconscious mind to do most of the heavy lifting. Any ideas that your subconscious mind learns, it feeds them to your ego. In order to avoid procrastination, you can make use of simple, but effective, techniques.

Plan out your day in advance, if possible. I don't mean that you have to plot every single action on a calendar. Rather, build a structure that incorporates all the important tasks that you have to do in a day. Sometimes, you might find out that you are unable to complete all the tasks, but that's okay, it's not a race or a deadline. As long as you're able to keep yourself occupied, you have accomplished your mission.

Don't keep distractions close to you and if possible, eliminate them entirely from your surroundings. For example, let's say that you're planning to lose weight. Avoid keeping any fat-filled or sugar-filled foods around you. Replace them with healthy alternatives.

Make sure you keep a priority journal where you record all the tasks and goals that are most important to you. Take a moment every day to go through the journal so you know what needs to take precedence for you. The constant reminders in the morning will encourage you not to slip into procrastination. In fact, even when you procrastinate, you will think about your journal and whether there are any pending tasks.

Hold yourself responsible. Make use of *Exercise #3: With Great Power Comes Great Responsibility* to help you accomplish this step.

Forgiveness

Remind yourself that you are merely human and that means you come with a bundle of faults and flaws. Then, forgive yourself for having those faults and flaws. It's okay to be imperfect, everyone is. By that, I mean everyone in the world. What's important is to acknowledge those imperfections and accept them. Forgive yourself for having them and then tell yourself that you are going to do better.

Then go ahead and become better.

Contentment

Create a routine in which you sit down to meditate every day. Use the simple breathing exercise in chapter six of this book to bring your mind to the present. After each session, devote a little time to thinking of the things in your life you are grateful for.

Indulge in the selfless act of gratitude and love. Think about how much you appreciate your friends and family. Be thankful for the small things. Congratulate yourself on the goals you have chosen to strive for. Yes, they might be quite challenging; but the fact is, you are a brave soul who has decided to make something out of yourself. Love your good qualities, the things you have, and the kindnesses you have shown others.

Take a look at your life and tell yourself that you have faced numerous challenges, all of which have eventually led you to this point. You are still here. You are still strong. You have already come this far and accomplished so much. You can still do it.

Gratitude

Thank the people in your life with honesty and openness. Let them know that you appreciate who they are and what they have done. I wouldn't recommend simply thanking to *appear* grateful. Rather, give thoughtful consideration to something that they have done for you recently and then genuinely, intentionally thank them for it.

Go ahead and thank strangers too. That barista who made your coffee? Offer a warm smile and give a wonderful thank you.

Rationality

Finally, apply rational thought and logic to your decisions. Don't do something just because you feel that it's the right thing. Ask yourself if it truly is the right choice. Look at the pros and cons. Evaluate the consequences. Conduct your own research.

Make informed decisions, and don't worry if it takes time to gather all the essential, necessary information. Remember the old adage, "measure twice and cut once." Armed with all the proper information, your decisions will be better positioned for success.

Conclusion

Alas, every journey has an end, and so your journey through this book has come to its eventual conclusion. But your journey towards improvement is just beginning. There are many miles in life to cover and numerous challenges to face. It's going to be quite the ride.

Before we part, I would like you to know that change is the driving force of life. It may not always pan out the way you want it to, and it might look scary at first. There are uncertainties to face and unexpected situations to encounter. But understand that change is vital. It is part of our lives, and there's no fighting it. Choose to ground yourself in reality and deal with the situations that arise with baby steps.

You will discover that eventually, and through consistency, you will walk the path of courage, self-confidence, and growth. You won't be afraid of taking risks. Fear won't stop you in your tracks and paralyze you. You will always turn towards looking for a solution rather than becoming overwhelmed with the problem.

Conclusion

Remember that it's okay if control slips from your hands. When that happens, you need only turn your attention to finding the most effective way to move forward. Evaluate your situation, try to look at all possible scenarios, look for help, and – more importantly – believe in yourself.

Both change and growth are vital fundamentals of life. Think of all the moments in your life that led you to becoming the person that you are. They all involved changes. Sure, some of those changes weren't pleasant at the time, but you still got through them. You made it here to be the splendid person that you are today.

From this point onwards, you don't have to be the person who sits passively by while change just happens to you. Instead, you can participate in those changes actively.

I may not be able to guarantee the results of your actions. No one can, for that matter. But what I can assure you is that you will discover even more opportunities, a lot more satisfaction, greater rewards, and a better sense of accomplishment. After all, growth and getting up every day to try your best is, in and of itself, still radical improvement. It takes a lot to have introspection and examine yourself; it's a vastly underrated quality. Moreover, you actually get to accomplish your goals. For without change, you are not going to be able to adapt to the situation at all.

Yes, you will have to adapt. You are not in control of absolutely everything that happens to you or to your goals. But that's okay. That's why you are going to become someone who is going to use change to your benefit.

Conclusion

I believe in your strength to become a spectacular person. I believe in your ability to grow and constantly transform into a better version of yourself.

I believe in your courage when it comes to dealing with change in your personal life. Therefore, it is my sincerest hope that you can use the tips and advice provided in this book to supplement your journey towards taking charge of a more intentional, fulfilling, courageous life. I know you can do it!

Thank you so much for taking the time to read this book, I hope you've enjoyed it. I would really appreciate it if you could help others to battle their fear of change by leaving a review on Amazon or at www.magletpublishing.com.

If you'd like to download a free SMART goals worksheet, head over to www.magletpublishing.com/smartgoals.

References

Abdallah, Chadi G, and Paul Geha. "Chronic Pain and Chronic Stress: Two Sides of the Same Coin?" Chronic Stress, vol. 1, Jan. 2017, p. 247054701770476, 10.1177/2470547017704763.

American Psychological Association. "APA Dictionary of Psychology." Dictionary.apa.org, dictionary.apa.org/locus-of-control.

"Apple First US Company to Be Valued at $2tn." BBC News, 19 Aug. 2020, www.bbc.com/news/business-53840471#:~:text=Tech%20giant%20Apple%20has%20become.

"Humans Wired to Be Lazy–Study." BBC News, 10 Sept. 2015, www.bbc.com/news/health-34198916. Accessed 18 July 2021.

Carleton, R. Nicholas. "Fear of the Unknown: One Fear to Rule Them All?" Journal of Anxiety Disorders, vol. 41, June 2016, pp. 5–21, 10.1016/j.janxdis.2016.03.011.

References

Colier, Nancy. "Negative Thinking: A Dangerous Addiction." Psychology Today, 15 Apr. 2019, www.psychologytoday.com/us/blog/inviting-monkey-tea/201904/negative-thinking-dangerous-addiction.

Douglas, Kate. "Picking Our Brains: How Powerful Is the Subconscious?" New Scientist, 30 Mar. 2010, www.newscientist.com/article/mg20627541-900-picking-our-brains-how-powerful-is-the-subconscious/. Accessed 22 July 2021.

Fell, Jason. "How Steve Jobs Saved Apple." Entrepreneur, 2011, www.entrepreneur.com/article/220604.

Ferrari, Joseph. "Psychology of Procrastination: Why People Put off Important Tasks until the Last Minute." Https://www.apa.org, 2010, www.apa.org/news/press/releases/2010/04/procrastination.

Hofmann, Stefan G., et al. "Neurobiological Correlates of Cognitions in Fear and Anxiety: A Cognitive–Neurobiological Information-Processing Model." Cognition & Emotion, vol. 26, no. 2, Feb. 2012, pp. 282–299, 10.1080/02699931.2011.579414.

Kanter, Rosabeth Moss. "Ten Reasons People Resist Change." Harvard Business Review, 26 Sept. 2018, hbr.org/2012/09/ten-reasons-people-resist-chang.

Kerr, Robert, et al. "Emotional Intelligence and Leadership Effectiveness." Leadership & Organization Development Journal, vol. 27, no. 4, June 2006, pp. 265–279, manajemenrumahsakit.net/wp-content/uploads/2012/09/EI-leadership-effectiveness.pdf, 10.1108/01437730610666028.

King's College London. "Do Negative Thoughts Increase Risk of Alzheimer's Disease?" Medicalxpress.com, 17 Nov. 2014,

References

medicalxpress.com/news/2014-11-negative-thoughts-alzheimer-disease.html.

Leahy, Robert. "Robert L. Leahy Ph.D. | Psychology Today." Www.psychologytoday.com, 8 May 2008, www.psychologytoday.com/us/contributors/robert-l-leahy-phd. Accessed 5 Aug. 2021.

Leary, Mark. "Getting to the Psychological Core of Humility | SPSP." Spsp.org, 5 Oct. 2020, spsp.org/news-center/blog/leary-psychology-humility. Accessed 10 Aug. 2021.

Marcin, Ashley. "Atychiphobia: Understanding Fear of Failure." Healthline, 18 Sept. 2018, www.healthline.com/health/atychiphobia.

Mead, Elaine. "Comfort Zones: An Alternative Perspective." Psych Central, 26 Nov. 2018, psychcentral.com/blog/comfort-zones-an-alternative-perspective#1.

Merriam-Webster. "Definition of CALAMITY." Www.merriam-Webster.com, www.merriam-webster.com/dictionary/calamity. Accessed 24 July 2021.

"Definition of CHANGE." Merriam-Webster.com, 2019, www.merriam-webster.com/dictionary/change.

"Definition of COMFORT ZONE." Merriam-Webster.com, 2020, www.merriam-webster.com/dictionary/comfort%20zone.

"Definition of CONFIDENCE." Www.merriam-Webster.com, www.merriam-webster.com/dictionary/confidence.

"Definition of COURAGE." Merriam-Webster.com, 2009, www.merriam-webster.com/dictionary/courage.

References

National Alliance on Mental Illness. "Anxiety Disorders." Nami.org, 2017, www.nami.org/About-Mental-Illness/Mental-Health-Conditions/Anxiety-Disorders.

Nickerson, Raymond S. "Confirmation Bias: A Ubiquitous Phenomenon in Many Guises." Review of General Psychology, vol. 2, no. 2, 1998, pp. 175–220, journals.sagepub.com/doi/10.1037/1089-2680.2.2.175, 10.1037/1089-2680.2.2.175.

Novotney, Amy. "The Risks of Social Isolation." Https://Www.apa.org, May 2019, www.apa.org/monitor/2019/05/ce-corner-isolation.

Razzetti, Gustavo. "How to Overcome the Fear of Change." Psychology Today, 2018, www.psychologytoday.com/us/blog/the-adaptive-mind/201809/how-overcome-the-fear-change.

Shusterman, Richard. "Muscle Memory and the Somaesthetic Pathologies of Everyday Life." Human Movement, vol. 12, no. 1, 1 Jan. 2011, www.degruyter.com/downloadpdf/j/humo.2011.12.issue-1/v10038-011-0001-2/v10038-011-0001-2.pdf, 10.2478/v10038-011-0001-2. Accessed 11 Aug. 2019.

Singh, Manoj. "The 2007-08 Financial Crisis in Review." Investopedia, 26 July 2020, www.investopedia.com/articles/economics/09/financial-crisis-review.asp.

Smithsonian National Museum of Natural History. "Social Life | the Smithsonian Institution's Human Origins Program." Humanorigins.si.edu, humanorigins.si.edu/human-characteristics/social-life?correlationId=ffc4ef19-e074-4d40-933b-6ca861ad4a27. Accessed 25 July 2021.

Taibbi, Robert. "Do You Have Analysis Paralysis?" Psychology Today, 24 Apr. 2019, www.psychologytoday.com/us/blog/fixing-families/201904/do-you-have-analysis-paralysis.

Tulving, E, and D. Schacter. "Priming and Human Memory Systems." Science, vol. 247, no. 4940, 19 Jan. 1990, pp. 301–306, 10.1126/science.2296719.

Warren, Cortney. "To Change or Not to Change | Psychology Today." Www.psychologytoday.com, 8 July 2014, www.psychologytoday.com/us/blog/naked-truth/201407/change-or-not-change. Accessed 31 July 2021.

Watts, Andrew. "Why Do We Develop Certain Irrational Phobias?" Scientific American Mind, vol. 25, no. 1, 19 Dec. 2013, pp. 74–74, www.scientificamerican.com/article/why-do-we-develop-certain-irrationa/, 10.1038/scientificamericanmind0114-74a.

Yang, Haiyang, et al. "Why We Set Unattainable Goals." Harvard Business Review, 4 Jan. 2021, hbr.org/2021/01/why-we-set-unattainable-goals. Accessed 18 July 2021.

Zaltman, Gerald, and Harvard Business Press. How Customers Think: Essential Insights into the Mind of the Market. Boston Massachussetts, Harvard Business School Press, Copyright, 2003.

www.ingramcontent.com/pod-product-compliance
Lightning Source LLC
Chambersburg PA
CBHW072057110526
44590CB00018B/3204